D1491331

THE OFFICIAL
DICTIONARY
OF
IDIOCY

STERLING
New York

An Imprint of Sterling Publishing Co., Inc.
1166 Avenue of the Americas
New York, NY 10036

STERLING and the distinctive Sterling logo are registered trademarks of
Sterling Publishing Co, Inc.

Text © 2018 James Napoli
Illustrations © 2018 Sterling Publishing Co., Inc.

All rights reserved. No part of this publication may be reproduced, stored
in a retrieval system, or transmitted in any form or by any means (including
electronic, mechanical, photocopying, recording, or otherwise) without prior
written permission from the publisher.

ISBN 978-1-4549-2780-8

Distributed in Canada by Sterling Publishing Co., Inc.
c/o Canadian Manda Group, 664 Annette Street
Toronto, Ontario, Canada M6S 2C8
Distributed in the United Kingdom by GMC Distribution Services
Castle Place, 166 High Street, Lewes, East Sussex, England BN7 1XU
Distributed in Australia by NewSouth Books
45 Beach Street, Coogee, NSW 2034, Australia

For information about custom editions, special sales, and premium and
corporate purchases, please contact Sterling Special Sales at 800-805-5489 or
specialsales@sterlingpublishing.com.

Manufactured in China

2 4 6 8 10 9 7 5 3 1

sterlingpublishing.com

Interior design by Gavin Motnyk
Illustrations by Alexis Seabrook

THE OFFICIAL
DICTIONARY
OF
IDIOCY

A Lexicon For Those of Us
Who Are Far Less Idiotic
Than the Rest of You

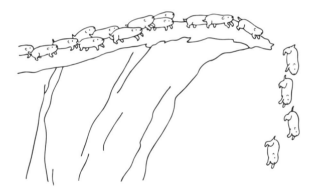

JAMES NAPOLI
Executive Vice President
National Sarcasm Society

STERLING
New York

ACK NOW LEDG MENTS

ACKNOWLEDGMENTS

So many people are integral parts of what it takes to write a book.

Yeah, right. How many people besides me were put to work like a farm ox on churning out snide definitions for more than a thousand everyday words and phrases? Zero, that's how many. Writing is a solitary endeavor.

So any of you friends and acquaintances who think they are going to get a nod for supporting me through this arduous process, or for slipping me a joke or two under the table, forget it. I didn't see you getting carpal tunnel ripping through the veneer of all we hold most dear.

And, no, wife and/or kids who want to lay claim to providing such a loving space in which to work, you shall not have your egos stroked, either. So, you took care of the chores a little more than usual or made a meal when I was too buried by deadlines to take care of myself. Big deal, I'd do the same for you, and would probably see through the hollow gesture of a pitiful mention in the acknowledgments section of your book as the lazy commemoration that it is.

Besides, the last thing anybody wants to read is a list of unfamiliar names in a book they bought for reasons far removed from curiosity about a group of eighteen people that are tangentially connected to the author in a variety of inconsequential ways. And I should know, since I am one of those jerks who feel compelled to read every stupid word of a book, including moronic sections like this.

That being said, there are a couple of people who could probably use a mention.

The significant contributions of *The Official Dictionary of Idiocy's* editor, Chris Barsanti, whose involvement in making many of the entries in this book a bit more understandable, and in the process making me feel like an idiot, should not go unheralded. The eagle eyes of the copy editor Phillip Gaskill further highlighted my idiotic tendencies by spotting such screw-ups as grammatical errors in the entries about my frustration with grammatical errors. One could look far and wide for a better example of confidence-shrinking humiliation and fail to find it. Cheers, everyone.

Finally, a tip of the hat to the American Library Association, whose poster in praise of the value of reading featured the cast of *The Big Bang Theory,* and in which Jim Parsons is depicted perusing *The Official Dictionary of Sarcasm,* the precursor to this very book. Some things you just can't be sarcastic about.

James Napoli
Executive Vice President
National Sarcasm Society

INTRODUCTION

INTRODUCTION

Idioting is not a word, at least according to my spell-check. But it should be, since what do idiots do all day if not a whole lot of idioting?

The idiots are everywhere. On your TV, in your public institutions, even sitting right there in your living room (sorry, loved ones). There are also several books that purport to guide idiots through the steps of various skill sets. And here is the most frightening statistic about idiocy there is: we've all exhibited it. I certainly see myself in several of the entries in this compendium and perhaps you, gentle reader, will see yourself in some of them as well. (Wait, what am I talking about? If you've decided to buy this book, you are anything but gentle.)

It is vital, when reading *The Official Dictionary of Idiocy*, to keep our own forays into the idiotic at the forefront of our consciousness, as we breeze through the alphabet taking in examples of all the *other* idiots whose behavior and thought processes make up the lion's share of these entries. Certainly, readers of this tome may be guilty of a few of the lapses in intelligence detailed here, but nowhere near as many as the unpardonable idiots with whom they are forced to deal on a daily, often hourly basis.

The key to enjoyment of this lexicon is to allow a very tiny portion of one's own fragile ego to give way, so that the sense of superiority over the vast majority of idiots will not seem so pronounced. After all, nobody likes an idiot who protests too much about not being an idiot.

Is there sarcasm on display here? Of course. I am, after all, Executive Vice-President of the National Sarcasm Society. (A title I never even knew existed until the publishers invented it for me amid the release of *The Official Dictionary of Sarcasm*, at which point I decided just to roll with the idiocy; how's that for irony?) But the starting point of each entry here is to inquire as to the idiotic nature of the words, phrases, people, and ideas with which we surround ourselves. That is, to borrow a phrase that did not make it into the dictionary but may well be worthy of it, its prime directive.

So, yes, we're all in here, and, that said, do enjoy this stroll down idiocy lane. And if it becomes too much to recognize the image of yourself in any of the definitions, then by all means recognize everyone else. You know, all those idiots who are the *real* idiots.

BY
THE
NUM
BERS

BY THE NUMBERS

9 TO 5: Eight hours of sheer idiocy. Ten if you count the commute.

10 ITEMS OR LESS: A sign that is so frequently and cavalierly ignored that it might as well be the pooping-dog-with-the-red-line-across-it placard in front of your neighbor's house.

15 MINUTES OF FAME: What Andy Warhol said everyone would achieve in the future. Had he only lived to see the Internet and Reality TV, he would have known that 15 minutes of idiocy would have been far more accurate.

24-HOUR NEWS CYCLE: Oh, please. Those tragic deaths, ideological warfare casualties, and examples of government malfeasance are *so* yesterday.

867-5309: Phone number from a 1980s song by Tommy Tutone that caused uncountable numbers of idiots to make life a living hell for women named Jenny.

90: If 50 is the new 30 and 80 is the new 50, then 90 is the new dead.

99 CENT STORE: The place where saving money means not being able to read the languages on the packaging.

AND NOW ... THE ALPHABET

ABUNDANCE: A sense of overflowing fullness that you are guaranteed to attain if you only open yourself up to it. Which is hard to do when you are trapped in the negative energy of hurling your empty beer can at people who say things like this.

ACCOUNTANT: The person you trust with all the confidential details of your finances, and who probably wouldn't be at all tempted to steal from you just because he or she has been steadily losing prodigious quantities of former clients to TurboTax.®

ACT AS IF: The idea that behaving like you have already gotten what you want will allow that thing to come to you. Works very well for those who imagine having already achieved being an insufferable prig.

ACTION MOVIE: When it grows up, it wants to be a ride.

ACTIONS: The things that speak louder than words. Which will one day leave everybody on the Internet completely screwed.

ACTOR: Profession pursued by that one popular dude in high school who is now working as a museum guard and makes you glad you stayed in the family electrician business.

ACQUI-HIRE: To swallow up a business with the sole intent of poaching its top-notch staff. Don't worry, they're not after you.

ACTRESS: Profession pursued by that one popular girl in high school who is now a hugely successful movie star with tons of plastic surgery and about to lose her kids in a drug-related custody battle and makes you glad you stayed in the family electrician business.

ADULTING: Cute little term used by people terrified to admit that they have been spending anywhere from 18 to 39 years childing.

ADVERTISING:

AN ENTRENCHED SYSTEM OF PROPAGANDA THAT TRICKS YOU INTO THINKING ANY NUMBER OF USELESS PRODUCTS WILL MAKE YOU LESS OF AN IDIOT THAN YOU ALREADY ARE.

AIRBNB: Lodging sharing service that lets you guess which of your gracious worldwide hosts will charge you the most monumentally disproportionate cleaning fee.

AIR CONDITIONING: Area cooling technology founded on the principle that there is absolutely no middle ground between a little too warm and Antarctica's Vostok Station.

AIRPLANE:

THE INEVITABLE RESPONSE TO MANKIND'S SUBCONSCIOUS NEED TO GET STUCK BEHIND SOME IDIOT TRYING TO LOAD A STEAMER TRUNK INTO AN OVERHEAD BIN.

AIRPORT: Travel hub wherein all the major airlines are encouraging everyone to use the automated check-in kiosks so that in just a few years' time there will be no more people around to complain to.

AIR QUOTES: A very annoying "gesture" that has "probably" polluted more "air" than greenhouse gas emissions.

ALARM CLOCK: The item that gets angrily slammed off in the first shot of every movie about a lovable deadbeat.

ALCOHOL: What we consume to take the pain away, while our sober friends wish they had something to take away the pain of dealing with idiots who use alcohol to take the pain away.

ALEXA: The entity one formally addresses when making a request of one's Amazon Echo device. And don't deny it: you know you have already found yourself hoping she likes you. *See also:* Siri.

ALEXANDER THE GREAT: Setting a lasting precedent for what humans truly value, this Macedonian king earned the term "great" by kicking the crap out of a lot of people and claiming their land as his own.

ALIEN: Either a being from another planet who you are convinced wants your stupid-ass body or a being from another country who you are convinced wants your stupid-ass job.

ALL YOU CAN EAT: A rather arrogant concept that is just begging for your local buffet to install a vomitorium.

ALTERNATIVE FACT: A way to justify living a lie that has proved so effective, it should be part of the marriage vows.

AMAZEBALLS: An exclamation of great wonder, arrived at with the questionable logic that adding balls to things is a generally good idea.

AMAZON.COM: The fulfillment of one of Nostradamus's lesser-known predictions, "One day, the people from whom you buy your adult diapers will also be responsible for making your TV shows."

AMAZON RAINFOREST: The largest tract of tropical rainforest in the world, with nearly 400 billion trees and a stunning array of species biodiversity. Like idiots like us could leave that alone. Come on.

AMERICAN DREAM, THE: Amorphous aspirational idea revolving around personal achievement and financial independence. Recently downgraded to The American Whimsical Notion.

AMERICA'S FUNNIEST HOME VIDEOS: *Masterpiece Theater* for idiots.

ANECDOTE: What idiots describe as an "antidote," almost as much as they describe astigmatism as "stigmata."

ANGER: The toxic result of feelings not expressed. And knowing that you failed to express your feelings should really piss you off.

ANGER MANAGEMENT: Therapeutic program that helps you redirect your anger into more positive channels. Let's start with punching yourself out, shall we?

ANGELS: Celestial beings you didn't give two craps about until you narrowly escaped death and became abruptly convinced that one of them suddenly decided to intervene on behalf of your agnostic ass.

ANIMALS: What idiots claim we all are whenever they want to rationalize their philandering.

ANNIVERSARY: The annual commemoration of an event, such as a great tragedy or a marriage. You see where this is going, right?

ANT: A creature roughly one one-thousandth the height of a human being with a brain the size of a nanoparticle that manages to be a million times better at creating a working societal model than we will ever be.

ANTI-PIRACY WARNINGS: The graphics that appear at the beginning of every DVD and Blu-ray and cannot be skipped over, resulting in a collective, worldwide time suck of 100 billion hours in just sitting there waiting for the root menu to kick in.

ANTIQUES ROADSHOW: The show you watch in dread, just knowing the dude that paid five bucks for that footstool at your yard sale will be sitting across from an appraiser who says it goes back to the Restoration era and is worth enough to pay off your house.

ANXIETY: Something you would have to be an idiot not to be constantly consumed by.

ANYTHING I CAN DO?: Idiotic phrase blurted out after a friend is injured or loses a loved one, and immediately tempered with the fervent hope that they will not take you up on your idiotic offer.

APATHY: A lack of engagement in the events that comprise one's life. Reflexively given a negative connotation by a bunch of idiots who can't seem to grasp that not giving a crap about anything is actually a damn fine way to get by.

APP: A program downloaded to one's mobile device. Oh, and the latest version of the Gold Rush, as millions of young people scurry to design some intensely practical or utterly inane thing that will feed enough smartphone addictions to buy them an ocean-view home and the lifelong jealous resentment of the few friends they manage to hold on to in the process.

APPLE:

A FRUIT THAT HAS BEEN INTERMARRIED INTO SO MANY DIFFERENT CRAZY VARIETIES THAT IT'S HARD TO BELIEVE THE TEA PARTY HASN'T TRIED TO PASS LEGISLATION AGAINST IT.

APRIL: Fourth month of the year, traditionally containing Easter, Passover, and the day your taxes are due. Yeah, okay, and God doesn't have a sense of humor?

ARGUMENT: Angry discussion over opposing viewpoints. You'd have to be an idiot to engage in this fruitless waste of time with anyone not in a position to provide make-up sex.

AROMATHERAPY: Infinitesimal amounts of scented oils that provide about as much therapy as your health plan.

ARROGANCE: The *Titanic*, with the power of speech.

ASSUMPTION: A belief or expectation that is accepted as true without the benefit of proof. Which leads to the question, "If God didn't want us to rush to make assumptions, why did he make them so much fun?"

ART:

A FORM OF SELF-EXPRESSION SO ESSENTIAL TO HUMAN DEVELOPMENT THAT IT IS THE FIRST THING TO GET AXED IN YOUR CHILD'S PUBLIC-SCHOOL CURRICULUM.

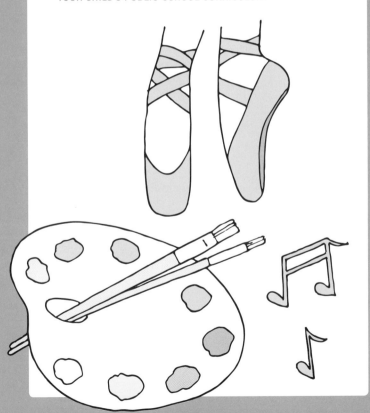

ASSISTED LIVING: Where we dump our parents when we can no longer assist in their living.

ATHEISTS: People leaving their decision about whether there is a supreme being in God's hands.

ATM: Cash-dispensing machine conveniently located at liquor stores, gambling establishments, and police stations, wherein the plan is to add insult to injury by tacking on a transaction fee to your alcoholic dependency, addiction to Texas Hold 'Em, or bail money.

AT THE END OF THE DAY: On one level, there is nothing intrinsically wrong with someone coming up with another way to say "When All is Said and Done." Therefore, it is difficult to explain why this particular corporate-speak buzz-phrase makes you wish you could drop an anvil onto the head of every idiot who comes out with it.

ATTENTION DEFICIT DISORDER: If you have it, you've already skipped to the B's.

ATTENTION WHORE: The adult equivalent of the 8-year-old who demands you sit through their excruciating *Moana*-inspired dance routine.

ATTRACTIVE: Set for life.

AUDIENCE: The rest of the people who shelled out good money for this crap.

AUDIOBOOK: The inevitable result of mankind's need to remove reading from the list of things one cannot do while multi-tasking.

AUGUST: Summer month containing the dog days, made even more galling by the fact that we cannot lick ourselves in public to cope with the heat.

AUTHENTIC: Something politicians always claim to be, even though the only authentic thing about politicians is how well they can fake authenticity.

AUTOMOBILE: A machine that allows idiots to rush about heedlessly from one place to another, barely slowing down to ask why they are engaged in such a relentless pursuit of futility. So, we're good, then.

AWESOME: Breathtaking; inspiring a daunting sense of impressiveness. Like completing a marathon in a wheelchair, or getting to level 100 in Candy Crush.

AWESOME SAUCE: See previous entry, add (for some inexplicable reason) sauce.

BABY:

A SMALLISH CREATURE IDIOTS KEEP AROUND TO ASSAULT MOVIE-THEATER AUDIENCES WITH UNGODLY SMELLS AND EAR-SPLITTING SOUNDS.

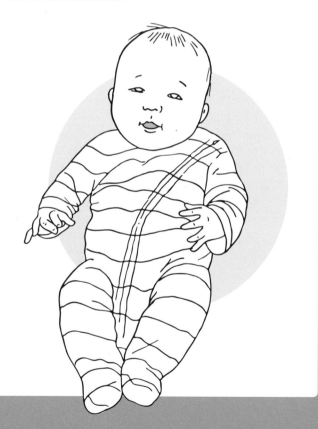

BACK TO THE FUTURE: Classic 1980s film. Sweet-natured sci-fi adventure comedy for the whole family about a guy who narrowly escapes having sex with his own mother. *See also:* Oedipus.

BA-DA-BOOM BA-DA-BING: Phrase derived from Italian-American culture that indicates one thing quickly leading to another. Such as a phrase from Italian-American culture being co-opted by a bunch of stunads and buttagaats who couldn't possibly do it justice. Fuggetaboutit.

BALLS: Something the world is so short of right now that it's surprising all its men aren't walking around singing falsetto.

BANDWAGON: A conveyance used by idiots to justify their every base desire and ill-conceived plan.

BANK: The place you leave your money so that businesses can do evil things with it while you await the day when you can use it to let the machines breathe for you.

BARBECUE: The backyard event at which the wearing of a novelty apron represents your poor, sad father's one and only excuse to cut loose.

BAR: The thing lawyers and alcoholics keep trying to pass.

BAR CODE: What your grandchildren will have branded into their foreheads at birth or, at the very latest, during the circumcision.

BARISTA:

IF YOU'RE GOING TO HAVE A MINIMUM-WAGE JOB, AT LEAST STRIVE TO HAVE THE ONE WITH THE COOLEST, MOST EUROPEAN-SOUNDING NAME.

BARS: The things that dictate the strength of a person's phone signal, or the things that keep a person in prison. I defy you to tell the difference.

BASEBALL:

NOT THE WORST WAY TO BORE YOURSELF SILLY FOR THREE HOURS, BUT IT WILL DO UNTIL THE WORST WAY GETS HERE.

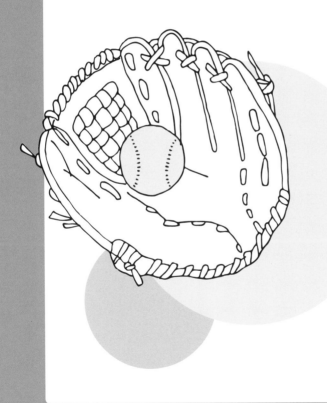

BASKETBALL:

A GREAT METAPHOR FOR LIFE. THAT IS, IF YOU CONSIDER
LIFE AN ENDLESS CYCLE OF RUNNING BACK AND FORTH
LOOKING FOR SOMEONE WHO'S OPEN WHILE YOUR
SNEAKERS MAKE PRONOUNCED
SQUEAKING NOISES ON
A PARQUET FLOOR.
WHICH YOU
PROBABLY DO.

BATHROOM: The location in one's home where idiots leave easily identifiable hairs behind as evidence of their crimes against humanity.

BEACH: The place where the exposed-flesh-to-desirable-exposed-flesh ratio is extremely low.

BEANIE: Also known as a stocking cap. The headgear worn by stoners in the middle of summer in order to make the rest of us shake our heads as to why anyone would wear a stocking cap in the middle of summer.

BED, BATH & BEYOND®: Home furnishings retailer whose definition of "beyond" is sadly confined to space organizers, picture frames, and potpourri.

BEEPS: The birdsong of the 21st century.

BEATLES: Legendary band who has made us pay for more useless remastered versions of their songs—that only sound vaguely different and are only of interest to idiots who care about minutiae like alternate takes and pre-roll chatter—than any other group of musicians in history.

BEES: Crucial and disappearing component of our ecosystem that may be signalling our downward spiral into extinction. So, anyway, which celebrity is in rehab again?

BEETHOVEN: Famous deaf composer who tragically never lived to hear it called hearing-impaired.

BEEYOTCH: A slightly more playful version of a derogatory term for a woman, broken into two syllables by another woman in order to communicate that the hatred is deep and all-consuming, but that she will probably stop short of the full-on scratching out of the eyes that is so tacitly implied by the one-syllable version.

BELT CLIP: As an alternative to the risk of leaving one's cell phone in a coffee shop, the belt clip is a highly practical accessory that is still not worth how dorky it makes you look.

BEST: What you give each and every day, knowing full well it will never be enough. Hard to believe this book could contain a more perfect example of idiocy than that. And we're only in the B's.

BESTIE: In probably a matter of weeks, your sworn enemy.

BEYONCÉ: Massive pop star whose inability to breathe without being hounded by idiots provides millions of young people with something to aspire to.

BFF: See "Bestie," add having to delete something like 33,000 photos from social media.

BIBLE:
EITHER A GENERIC TERM FOR A HEAVY BOOK OF RULES AND PROCEDURES OR SPECIFICALLY THE HOLY BIBLE, WHICH SUPPOSEDLY CONTAINS THE WORD OF GOD IN HISTORIC PARABLES. EITHER WAY, IDIOTS TEND TO HAVE OPINIONS ABOUT HOW *THEIR* BIBLE CAN BE USED TO SCREW ENTIRE SUBSETS OF PEOPLE OUT OF A HAPPY LIFE.

BIG LEBOWSKI, THE:
Cult film about a stoner that achieved its cult status by earning repeated viewings from people who couldn't remember seeing it the first time.

BIG PHARMA: Companies who make life-saving medicines and will kill you if you ask how.

BIG PICTURE, THE: What people who are about to create a policy that will ruin your entire life always encourage you to look at.

BIGLY: Nope. Not a word. Doesn't belong in a dictionary. We really should have deleted this.

BILL OF RIGHTS: The U.S. government's official designation of which citizens will be denied a bunch of things.

BILLIONAIRES: The people who control everything that affects our lives. They get a big kick out of all the working-class idiots who still believe they have a shot at joining their ranks.

BINGE WATCHING: An obsessive form of television viewing that creates such compulsion to keep going on that it might just stave off death.

BINGE-WORTHY: Designation for a television program that might merit a marathon viewing session of many continuous hours. Of course, ideas about which programs fit this description are subjective. But as a general rule, be wary of the oft-repeated "you just have to get through the first three episodes," which, let's face it, does not really qualify as a ringing endorsement.

BINGO: A game of chance that tells your family you are ready to end it all even more effectively than that Do Not Resuscitate paperwork.

BIRDSONG: The joyful utterings of nature's winged beings, heard as they greet each moment with a hymn to the universe, even though the stupid things only have a lifespan of, like, a minute.

BIRTHDAY: A date that brings up many different feelings in many different people. But everyone agrees on one thing: it was not meant to be commemorated by having wait-staff idiots surround your table and sing while you shrink into an awkward, humiliated heap.

BITCOIN:
A FORM OF VIRTUAL CURRENCY THAT'S THE ONLY THING MORE IDIOTIC THAN CONDUCTING BUSINESS WITH LITTLE SCRAPS OF PAPER AND PLASTIC CARDS WHICH WE ALL PRETEND ARE WORTH SOMETHING.

BLACK AND WHITE: Either a way of seeing things as simplistically good and bad, or an old movie shot without the benefit of color film. Weirdly, it wasn't until the latter went away that movies really started handing us the former.

BLAME: Something we must be careful not to assign to our parents as we take responsibility for our own shortcomings as adults. No, our parents are simply unconscious, deeply screwed-up individuals who are sooooo damn lucky they are not getting blamed right now.

BLESS YOU: Common nicety uttered after someone sneezes. Has its origins in the 6th century, when Pope Gregory the Great reportedly offered it as consolation to those whose sneeze might have indicated the onset of bubonic plague. Remember that, idiots, the next time you get all bent out of shape because your sweetheart forgets to acknowledge your commonplace little expulsion of air from the nostrils.

BLESSING IN DISGUISE: Something good coming out of something bad. Usually takes a really long time to reveal itself, if indeed it ever does, but we idiots are a hopeful lot.

BLING: Hard to say where jewelry crosses from ornamental to bling, but just as a general barometer, if your necklaces weigh more than your car, you're getting there.

BLOGS: Internet journals we maintain especially for those times when we need to reassure ourselves that nobody cares.

BLOOD: Oxygen-carrying liquid that flows through all our veins, no matter what our race or creed. I guess sometimes we need to see it spilling just to confirm this. No big deal.

BLOOD PRESSURE: What you check in that machine in the pharmacy while waiting for a refill on the medications used to treat your other life-threatening shortcomings.

BLU-RAY: Digital entertainment technology designed for those who insist that their meaningless drivel be presented at a resolution of 2160p.

BOAT: The ultimate symbol of hubris, a shameless drain on your finances that rots away in drydock and is exhumed once a year so you can show your drunken friends a good time on something they would never be so idiotic as to purchase.

BODY ODOR: A perfectly natural outgrowth of human activity we are so desperate to hide that we spread potentially cancer-causing substances on our underarms on a daily basis.

BOOK:
THE 8-TRACK TAPE OF READING.

BOOK CLUB: A group of people who have been gathering to discuss *Infinite Jest* for the past eleven years while secretly reading murder mysteries in the privacy of their own homes.

BOOT CAMP: In an insult to servicemen and women everywhere who have to slog through this grueling process, a term used to describe everything from an intense yoga workout to a seminar on how to be an effective Subway franchise manager.

BORDERS: Imaginary idiotic lines drawn between nations that conveniently provide all manner of excuses for us to kill each other.

BOT: An automated entity on the Internet that mimics interactions with users of various social-media networks. And, sadly, usually about eight times more intelligent than the users themselves.

BOTOX: Drug injection that reduces wrinkles by temporarily paralyzing facial muscles and good judgment.

BOUNCE HOUSE: Inflatable daycare center into which you deliberately toss your small, screaming children to be left under the reassuringly watchful eye of two dozen other small, screaming children while you go drink with the grownups.

BOUNCER: Sort of like a Secret Service agent if a Secret Service agent had to card underage drinkers instead of saving the President's life.

BOXER BRIEFS: Items that should not, repeat not, be entirely visible *while wearing pants*. That sh*t's getting old.

BOXING DAY: The day after Christmas. And round one for the idiots who leave their Christmas trees on the sidewalk to become brittle, long-dead, and diarrhea-colored while waiting for someone to magically make them disappear.

BOY:
NOT YET A MAN,
NO LONGER A FETUS.

BRAND: A highly recognizable set of attitudes and outlooks associated with a product. Once exclusive to corporations and businesses, now each and every person is apparently a brand, too, little realizing that their every tiny action contributes to the credibility of the image they present to the world. Is it any wonder that the term reminds one of having a logo seared into one's ass with a hot iron?

BRAND LOYALTY: An illusion clung to by idiots who believe that it actually matters where they buy the things they don't need.

BREAD: Since the beginning of time, a deeply felt symbol for the most basic of human nutritional needs. Now yet another thing we are not allowed to have because of the gluten or the carbs that break down as sugar or whatever. Yo, Jesus, if you come back, don't bother with the miracle of the loaves.

BREAKFAST: The meal that fast-food restaurants very thoughtfully make just as dangerously unhealthful as the rest of the menu.

BREAD BAG CLIP: The twist-tie or piece of plastic that seals your store-bought loaf of bread. And if forgetting where you set these damn things down two seconds after you open the bag is a sign of senility, then we've all been senile since were 21.

BREAKING NEWS: A term cable news stations use to label everything from the outbreak of war to the sighting of a Kardashian anytime, anywhere.

BREATHING: The act of taking air into and out of the lungs. Sometimes the perspective one can gain from simply taking a slow, calming breath can be so illuminating about who we really are that we will never, ever do it again.

BRING IT ON: Boastful phrase used by idiots who have no idea how badly they are about to be beaten.

BRO: Overly broad term of endearment used to greet roughly six actual brothers in the last thirty years.

BROMANCE: A way for guys to admit that they would kill to sleep with one another, but without all the hassle of saying that they would kill to sleep with one another.

BUFFET, WARREN: Famously decent and philanthropic rich person who sets a dangerous precedent for the rest of us idiots—who have always hoped to become indecent and self-serving rich people.

BUCK NAKED: The only way to describe being completely naked, despite the idiots from the "butt naked" camp who insist on offending your delicate sensibilities.

BUDGET: What you kick yourself for never being able to balance, while trying to forget the fact that the nation's finances are in the hands of way bigger idiots than you.

BUILD-YOUR-OWN: Idiotic concept preying on the human illusion of control that somehow caught on in the hamburger and pizza universe even though the ostensible translation of "Build Your Own" is pretty much "Um, yeah, give me that, that, and that."

BULLET POINTS: A list of the most relevant and achievable aspects of any given topic. And absolute hell to reformat.

BUMPER STICKER: Handy way to make your political beliefs known on the rear of your car, so that any mentally unstable nut job who wants to ram you with the front of theirs will have even more cause to do so.

BUREAUCRATS: The men and women who run all the government programs and institutions that bureaucrat-hating idiots rely on to stay alive.

BURNING MAN: Once a grassroots gathering of counterculture iconoclasts, now a big-ticket gathering of only the authentic, starving artist bohemians who can quickly put their hands on thousands of dollars of disposable income.

BURRITO: The most ill-advised first-date food known to mankind.

BUSINESS: The stuff that has been sadly proceeding "as usual" since we first learned to walk erect.

BUTTER: Dairy product that tried for a very long time to hide from the idiots who wanted to deep-fry it.

CABLE NEWS: Trusted information source for people who believe news is best delivered by idiots shouting opinions over each other.

CABLE TELEVISION: Bloated, overpriced provider of hundreds of entertainment channels we don't need but makes it all worthwhile for Turner Classic Movies.

CAFETERIA: Dining that involves doling out food onto a tray and then looking up at the available tables to see if anyone will let you sit with them without demeaning your budding sense of sexuality or beating the living crap out of you. Wait, you did say *junior high school cafeteria*, right?

CAFFEINE: What you need in the morning to get you going because you didn't sleep because you needed it in the afternoon to keep you going.

CAKE: Something that you cannot have and eat, making it a symbol of ineffable loss. Delicious, delicious loss.

CALENDAR: Charming device that maps out our lives into constrictive blocks, thus trapping us in a world of commitments and appointments from which there is no escape save death. Don't know what we'd do without it.

CALIGULA: Notoriously debauched Roman Emperor from 37 to 41 A.D. So absurd was his reign that he apparently made his horse a Senator. Idiotic, right? Hey, wait a minute, maybe we could learn something here.

CANADA:

THE PLACE TO WHICH IDIOTS IN THE UNITED STATES THREATEN TO MOVE EVERY TIME A REACTIONARY TAKES OFFICE, LITTLE REALIZING THAT CANADA HAS PLENTY OF IDIOTS OF ITS OWN AND DOES NOT NEED ANY MORE DRAINS ON THEIR FREE HEALTH-CARE SYSTEM.

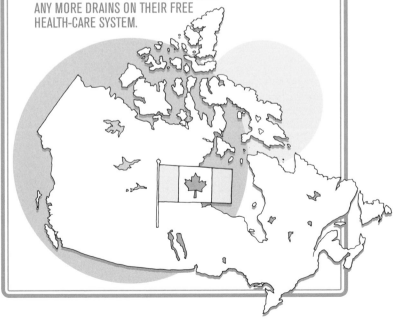

CAR ALARM: Anti-theft device that makes your neighbors *hope* your car is being stolen.

CARE: What you say you do when you know you don't. Admit it.

CARLIN, GEORGE: Never mind Jesus. This is the guy we need to come back and take names.

CASHIER: A person who would not know what a nectarine was without consulting the little UPC sticky label attached to it.

CASKET: The container in which you are buried that costs more than the mortgage on the container you spent your time in while alive.

CASUAL FRIDAY: A concept born of the notion that being able to wear jeans once a week will compensate for years of under-appreciation, idiotic tasks, and thinly veiled jabs at your self-esteem.

CAT:

THE ONLY LIVING CREATURE CAPABLE OF HAVING MORE UTTER CONTEMPT FOR YOU, WHILE ALSO SLEEPING AWAY HALF THE DAY, THAN YOUR SULLEN TEENAGER.

CATFIGHT: Two or more women pummeling each other. An occurrence purported to turn men on, as if the sight of two or more men pummeling each other doesn't get them equally, if not more, turned on.

CATFISH: To lure someone in with a fake Internet persona. Oh, please. Like we all aren't doing that already.

CEILING: The thing you have stared up at hopelessly during more sexual encounters with idiots than you care to remember.

CELL PHONE: An expensive and hard-to-replace item that characters in movies never think twice about shattering when frustrated.

CENTENARIANS: Those poor saps who have lived through a hundred years of the idiocy you are currently experiencing.

CEO: The idiot who makes on average 204 times more than the other idiots who think such a discrepancy is perfectly okay.

CEREAL: Breakfast food that rushes to tell us it is vitamin-fortified in rather the same way that a doctor has us sign the release before we get on the treadmill.

CGI: 1. Computer Generated Imagery. 2. Hollywood-speak to indicate the conspicuous lack of a compelling narrative.

CHANGE: What each of us must achieve if we are to evolve as human beings; what none of us can ever achieve because there are just too many other idiots to blame for us not achieving it.

CHANNEL SURFING: Zen meditation for the chronically unemployed.

CHARMING: Preparing the crawlspace.

CHECKOUT LINE: A galling two-foot-long stretch of wire racks featuring all the luscious candy items that make you fat, right next to the magazines shaming you for how fat you are.

CHEESE:

IT DOESN'T MATTER HOW MUCH YOUR HOME STATE RELIES ON ITS DAIRY-RICH ECONOMY TO SURVIVE, THERE IS SIMPLY NO EXCUSE FOR WEARING A GIANT FOAM REPLICA OF THIS FOOD PRODUCT ON YOUR DAMN HEAD.

CHEMTRAIL:
SKYWRITING FOR THE PARANOID.

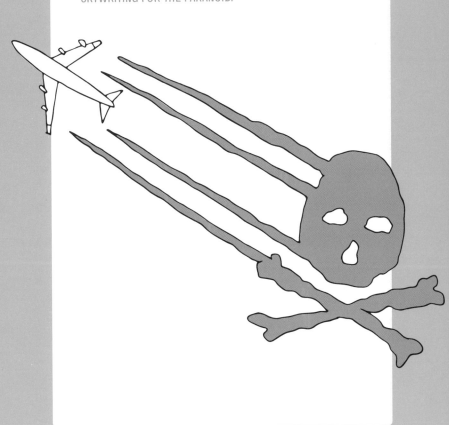

CHEW TOY: The pet accessory that most dog owners would totally play with if no one was looking.

CHILDREN: Tiny versions of ourselves whom we refuse to discipline, and we worship so unconditionally that we might as well call it a day and give them their own church.

CHILL: Relaxed. Easygoing. Unconcerned. With the fact that you just used the word "chill."

CHOICE: A concept we idiots think we are exercising on a daily basis, as if who we sleep with, what coffee we like, or what stock offering we got in on the ground floor of is going to make a sh*t's bit of difference when we are dead.

CHOIR: What you are preaching to. So please just stop.

CHOMSKY, NOAM: Famous left-wing rabble-rouser whose name is synonymous with radical thought. He would be a far more terrifying figure to those on the right if the word "thought" indicated anything in which Americans were still engaged.

CHRISTMAS:
A HOLIDAY INSPIRED BY JESUS CHRIST'S LITTLE-KNOWN BUT INCREDIBLY POWERFUL PARABLE *THE BLIND MAN AND THE CONSUMER-DRIVEN ECONOMY.*

CHRISTMAS PARTY: The event at which your workplace gives you the chance to mingle awkwardly with the fifteen employees who just learned they will be canned in the New Year.

CHRONIC FATIGUE: Perhaps not as deadly as the bubonic plague, but for anyone who has tried to stay ahead of the bills in the 21st century, certainly the cause of a very different type of dropping dead.

CIGARETTES: Products created so that those with a death wish can at least experience full, rich tobacco flavor on their way to the grave.

CINCO DE MAYO: Not that white guys needed another holiday they know nothing about to use as a springboard into getting hammered, but hey, they aren't complaining.

CIRQUE DU SOLEIL: Talented group of acrobats and contortionists that has everyone breathlessly anticipating when they are going to use *The Silence of the Lambs* for inspiration.

CLASS-ACTION LAWSUIT: The only form of advertising left on terrestrial TV.

CLASSIC ROCK: The stuff that plays in nursing homes now.

CLICKBAIT: A link to a trivial but titillating item on the Internet that users find very difficult to resist. Also known as a link to any given item on the Internet.

CLIMATE CHANGE: Something the few remaining polar bears, though pointedly incapable of reasoning or speech, are well aware of. Even as millions of idiots who have the ability to figure stuff out, and even talk, insist on acting like dumb animals.

CLOUDS: Natural formations that we allow to darken our mood whenever they blot out the sun or rain and snow on us. The last time we gave over that much of our power to a puffy white thing, look what happened.

COFFEE: The only highly addictive substance that comes with the option of low-foam.

COLLEGE: Where students go after high school to major in debt.

COLLEGE RADIO: Your trusted source for three-hour blocs of refrigerator hum.

COLOGNE: A substance men splash on liberally in the belief that the sting it will give their lover's nostrils will cause a distraction from the largely inadequate sexual encounter they are providing.

COLUMBUS, CHRISTOPHER: Not the first exploiter of indigenous people to become a hero, but certainly the first one who got us a Monday off.

COMIC CON: A place where hundreds of thousands of hopeless nerds could finally get laid if they weren't all dressed up in the awkward and impenetrable body armor of their favorite superheroes.

COMMENTS: The sections of the Internet that news organizations set aside to allow aspiring serial killers to make their views known.

COMMERCIALS: That they are three times louder in volume than the television programming they constantly interrupt might be more objectionable if they were not also three times more entertaining than the television programming they constantly interrupt.

COMMON COURTESY: Something that is about as common as a dot-matrix printer.

COMMUNITY: The warm and inspiring group of people with whom you are forced to develop a lasting fellowship based on the flimsy little fact that they live near you and show up at all the same stupid church events.

COMMUNITY COLLEGE: The place you decide to go after high school so that you can spend two years applying yourself to your studies before heading to a real college where you can party and puke your guts out for the remainder of your time in higher education.

COMMUNITY SERVICE: Volunteer work done to assist those in need in your area, and such an unbelievable pain in the ass that you only have to do it if you've broken the law and need to suddenly behave like a half-decent person in order to avoid going to prison.

COMPETITIVE: A personality trait that conveniently becomes the fall-back position of every idiot who pulls a mood when they lose.

COMPLAINTS: The section of a department store or workplace where a customer's or employee's voice can sink into a cavernous, unceasing hole of ignore.

COMPROMISE: The foundation of all successful marriages and affairs of state. Which is why a crap ton of marriages end in divorce and a crap ton of affairs of state end in bloodshed.

COMPUTER: A technological advance that has become such a ubiquitous part of our lives that we are probably using it to Google "ubiquitous" right now.

CONCERT: Music performed before a live audience. With classical music, the likely audience response is to fall asleep from boredom. With concerts featuring classic rock bands of bygone eras, however, the likely audience response is to fall asleep from old age. *See also: Classic Rock.*

CONFABULATE: To fabricate imaginary experiences as overcompensation for loss of memory. Damn, if we all really are just somebody's dream, we've been confabulated up the wazoo.

CONFEDERATE FLAG: Controversial emblem that so many people see as a symbol of repression and racial inequality that it's readily available in handy bumper-sticker form.

CONGRESS:

THE ONLY GROUP OF PEOPLE WHO GIVE LESS OF A CRAP
ABOUT YOU THAN YOUR FAMILY DOES.

CONSERVATIVE: People whose passion for their
traditional view of how the world should work is
completely dwarfed by the passionate hatred they feel
for those who don't see it that way. *See also:* Liberal.

CONSPIRACY:

AN ATTEMPT BY THE GOVERNMENT TO HIDE THE TRUTH ABOUT SOMETHING NASTY BY SETTING IN MOTION AN INCREDIBLY INTRICATE, LABYRINTHINE SERIES OF EVENTS THAT THE IDIOTS WHO MAKE UP YOUR GOVERNMENT WOULD NOT BE CAPABLE OF IN A MILLION YEARS.

CONSTITUTION, THE: Aside from those lame Hollywood scripts based on old TV shows, the single most rewritten document in history.

CONSUMERS: The final, desperate pillars holding up a crumbling service-based economy that must either undergo an enormous paradigm shift or be trampled under the boot of the very countries we allowed to surpass us by paying them to crank out cheaper versions of all the crap we used to make ourselves.

CONTACT LIST: The feature of your phone that has handily killed your ability to remember a single telephone number ever again.

CONTENT CREATOR:

FANCY NAME FOR A WRITER. IN THE CASE OF TELEVISION PROGRAMS, SOMEONE WHO IS PAID MILLIONS TO CREATE CONTENT. IN THE CASE OF A BLOGGER, SOMEONE WHO IS PAID NOTHING TO CREATE CONTENT. IN THE CASE OF THE AUTHORS OF SATIRICAL DICTIONARIES, SOMEONE WHO IS ONE STEP UP FROM A BLOGGER.

CONTEXT: Oh, honestly, who has the time?

CONTRACTOR: A person you throw your life savings at while he stands there with a tape measure clipped to his belt.

CONTROL: Asserting dominance over a situation in order to have an impact on its outcome. Routinely stymied by floods, hurricanes, death, and where your spouse would rather go for dinner.

CONTROL FREAK: A person who feels compelled to take command of every circumstance. Routinely stymied by running out of circumstances to control by virtue of running out of friends who don't want to kill them.

CONVERSATION: What the Internet always claims to make you a part of, while ignoring the fact that rating a gas grill on Amazon or ranting about the ineffectuality of an argument on *Huffington Post* does not exactly vault you into the freaking Algonquin Round Table.

CONVERSION THERAPY:

A FORM OF PSYCHOLOGICAL COUNSELING DESIGNED BY IDIOTS IN THE HOPES OF REORIENTING ONE'S SEXUAL PREFERENCE. THE AMOUNT OF HETEROSEXUALS WHO COULD PROBABLY BENEFIT FROM THIS NONSENSE HAS NOT YET BEEN ACCURATELY MEASURED.

CORE COMPETENCIES: Da things ya do good at. There, was that so hard, Mr. Buzzword inventor?

CORNERS: You know, those things that the people in charge of your town cut all the time, resulting in everything from wrongful-death lawsuits to the far more troubling substandard post office experience.

CORPORATION: Business entity that was declared a person a while back. Which is only fair, since corporations really should have the same rights as any other normal person who can put their hands on eight billion dollars with a single phone call.

COSPLAY: Dressing up as a character from manga or anime. As alienating your parents goes, it's probably preferable to doing hard drugs or selling your body in an alley.

COUCH POTATO: A person who has finally discovered that they are going to die whether they exercise or not.

COUGH:

SOMETHING WE ARE NOW SUPPOSED TO DO INTO OUR ELBOWS, EVEN THOUGH WE LOOK LIKE TOTAL DOUCHEBAGS DOING IT.

COUNTER-INTUITIVE: Working against the brain's natural instincts. Commonly seen in pull-down menus and the choosing of a life partner.

COUNTRY MUSIC:

SONGS ABOUT SIMPLE FOLKS ENJOYING
BEERS, BARBECUES, AND OLD-
FASHIONED VALUES SUNG
BY PHILANDERING MULTI-
MILLIONAIRES WHO WOULD
NOT BE CAUGHT DEAD
SHARING A BREWSKI WITH
THE BURGER-FLIPPING HICKS
WHO PAY THEIR RENT.

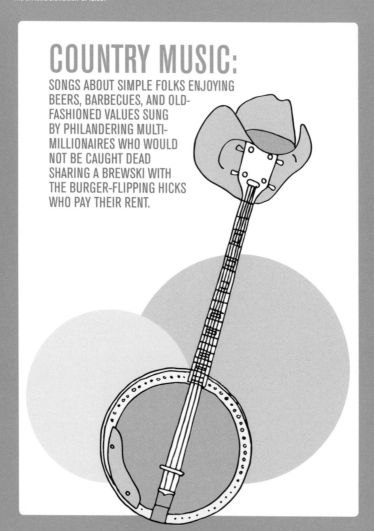

COUPONS: Reportedly money-saving bits of paper employed by idiots who are under the delusion that the retailer hasn't already come out ahead anyway.

COURAGE: In its purest form, courage is not the absence of fear, but the ability to control one's bladder in the face of fear.

COW: An animal that we punish for producing greenhouse gases with its farts by killing and eating it.

CO-WORKER: A person with whom you have virtually nothing in common, aside from a mutual feeling of hatred and resentment for the job you are both forced to do, and every other soul-sucking moron you are forced to do it with. If that's not the foundation of a lifelong friendship, I don't know what is.

CRAIGSLIST: The place where your date, your modular wall unit, and your job interview are all of roughly the same quality.

CRAY: Slang term for "crazy," created when the human race finally realized that two-syllable words were simply becoming far too inconvenient.

CREDIT CARD: The reason you are currently giving sexual favors for five bucks a pop.

CRIME:

A CONDITION WE'RE SO EAGER TO PREVENT THAT WE ESCHEW ALL FORMS OF PREVENTION AND LET CORPORATIONS RUN OUR PRISON SYSTEM LIKE HOTEL CHAINS. ALBEIT HOTEL CHAINS WITH SOUL-DESTROYING, DEHUMANIZING VIOLENCE THAT INVOLVES THE CONCEPT OF PREVENTION ABOUT AS MUCH AS A BROKEN CONDOM.

CRITICAL THINKING: Not sure. Used to know what that meant. Hm. Let me get back to you.

CROSS-TRAINING: Aptly-named multi-disciplinary approach to athletics that metaphorically hoists its practitioners onto a cross so all their friends can see how much suffering is involved in being a badass.

CROSSWALK: An area of a roadway set aside for pedestrians, so that they may risk their lives.

CROW: A bird whose vast storehouse of intelligence includes being able to plan, solve complex problems, and even remember human faces. One cannot help but think that in a Crow vs. The Incumbent election, the Incumbent would lose by a landslide.

CROWDFUNDING: Getting a bunch of suckers to shell out for your pipe dream. *See also: Kickstarter.*

CRUISE: The only all-you-can-eat buffet that could result in drowning.

CRUSH: 1. To pulverize with forceful compression. 2. To mercilessly defeat an opponent. 3. To be romantically infatuated with an unattainable person, which could lead to both merciless defeat and pulverizing by forceful compression, depending upon how far you take things.

CRYING: An emotional release that you know you must have needed for a long time when it suddenly occurs unbidden during *Deadpool*.

CUBICLE: A prison cell that offers you the gut-wrenching ignominy of being allowed to leave it once a day.

CUCKSERVATIVE: Derogatory term for a conservative who secretly adheres to a largely more liberal agenda. Derives from the term "cuckold," which means it can only be understood by conservatives who secretly adhere to a largely more liberal agenda.

CULT: What you join when you have no other way of telling your parents that they should have held you a touch more accountable.

CULTURE: Either the collective representation of the arts in society or a scientific specimen that cultivates bacteria for analysis. If the user reviews on Netflix are any indication, the former can very easily resemble the latter.

CURMUDGEON: An ill-tempered, cantankerous old fellow who sees nothing of any value occurring in the world. They bug us because they get it.

CURRY: A word that is used to describe both a spicy turmeric rice dish and the idea of trying to ingratiate oneself to another by being obsequious. Clearly, somewhere along the line someone got a promotion by bringing in Indian food.

CYBERSPACE: The imaginary landscape over which communication via computer occurs. And if this definition is seen as implying that most of us now live in an imaginary landscape, well, there you go.

CYCLIST: An idiot who believes that a sign bearing the legend *Share the Road* means they will not be run over.

DAD:

TAKE IDIOT; ADD
CRAPLOADS OF UNWANTED
RESPONSIBILITY.

DANCE:

AN ACTIVITY DURING WHICH
EVERYBODY LOOKS LIKE AN IDIOT,
AND HENCE HUMANITY'S ONE
CHANCE TO REALIZE WE ARE ALL
THE SAME.

DANCE LIKE NO ONE IS WATCHING: And see how far you get before you feel like a total idiot. (See previous entry.)

DARK: Overused term used to describe entertainment content that treads into unsavory areas. Usually employed by people whose entire exposure to "dark" consists of that one time they had to use a Porta Potty.

DARWIN, CHARLES: Either an idiot, or a person thought of as an idiot by idiots, depending upon how willing you are to see the resemblances between yourself and a chimpanzee.

DATA PLAN: The reason you cannot afford drugs anymore.

DAY CARE: Where your children learn that, during the day, only other people care about them.

DAY JOB: What you have been urged not to quit so often that the concept of giving up the folk-singer dream might finally be sinking in.

DAYLIGHT SAVINGS: An opportunity to take advantage of longer days; to be outside in the light and walk among people. Wait, outside? With other people? No, God, please, no, not other people? How do I do that? What if they want to interact with me? Please let it get dark earlier again soon so I can spend more time with my smartphone.

DEAD: Something you realize you are not each morning. And, let's face it, idiots, most days that's a pretty good start.

DEADLINE: A cutoff point at which a project must be completed. Rather implies you're dead if you don't meet it, which is great because we need heart attacks to control the population.

DEATH: A sobering reminder that you should have thrown out all your crap instead of leaving it for your siblings to run down the chute into a dumpster.

DEBATE: Screaming match.

DEBIT CARD: You can swipe it. You can tap it. You can insert it. Yep, money is obscene all right.

DEBT:

IF THERE WERE SOMETHING THAT HAS SOMEHOW BECOME MORE INDISPENSABLE TO OUR EXISTENCE THAN AIR, THIS WOULD BE IT.

DECEMBER: The month when you finally have to admit you are bailing on every single one of your New Year's resolutions.

DELETE: The keystroke on your computer that waits patiently for you to employ it even as you consistently choose to enter a world of hurt by clicking SEND instead.

DEMOCRACY: An interesting idea that may one day take hold.

DEPLORABLE: A word used to describe something awful and utterly insulting to the very idea of being human. And, let's face it, some of the best "who's the baby daddy?" afternoon talk-show entertainment in the freaking world.

DEPRESSED: A state of general despondency that you really should get with the program and experience if you want to be like the rest of us.

DESCARTES, RENÉ: Father of Western philosophy, and famous for the maxim "cogito ergo sum," commonly translated as "I think, therefore I am." Sadly, if poor old René could see the moribund level of thinking being done in the 21st century, he would probably declare that we no longer am.

DESIDERATA: Famous prose poem that urges us to go placidly amid the noise and haste and watch as all those type-A personalities who couldn't go placidly amid the noise and haste if their lives depended on it get all the cash and glory.

DESIGNATED DRIVER: Someone who proudly takes on the responsibility of saving their drunken friend's life night after night but doesn't have the stones to tell the drunken friend that they need to get their stupid drunken act together before they push their car off a cliff with them in it.

DESIRE: A fervent craving or wish for something, which the Second Noble Truth of Buddhism holds is the basis for all human suffering. I fervently wish this weren't true.

DETACH: What we are encouraged to do from difficult personalities or situations. And if it helps to picture the idiot in question doing a death-tumble into space after you have "detached" him or her from the space pod, then by all means go there.

DEVICE: Generic term for whatever computer-based technology one has at one's disposal. And seeing as you have not yet looked up from your Fitbit, laptop, or smartphone, I think we will leave you to your own devices.

DEVIL'S ADVOCATE: The person who always brings the room down with the truth.

DICK PIC: A photograph of one's penis, usually as sent to an unwilling subject via email or social networking. All we can do is hope and pray that you-know-who will get caught doing this.

DICTATOR: A despotic head of state who represses and terrorizes his subjects, often to the point of having them killed when they disagree with him. So, privileged teenage kids: using this term to describe the parent who grounds you for partying too hard is idiotic hyperbole of the highest order.

DIFFERENT: Anything that confronts an idiot with the fact that we are all the same.

DIFFICULT: A useful word to employ when "pain in the ass" has already been taken.

DINNER: What idiots pay for in the mistaken belief that it entitles them to sex.

DIRECTOR: The person who points to where the explosions will happen.

DISAPPOINTMENT: What you are to your parents, largely because they were a couple of idiots who never lived their dreams and were hoping you would do it for them.

DISEASE: Any of countless disorders in the function of an organism that can threaten its survival. A good percentage of disease is preventable with exercise and a more sensible diet, but what fun is that?

DISINFORMATION: The spreading of lies in order to bait and perplex the public. The people responsible for this are one kind of idiot, and the people who fall for it are another kind of idiot altogether.

DISORDER: A word that can now be tacked onto the end of virtually any combination of other words to create the need for a side effects-laden pharmaceutical that can treat it.

DL, THE: The down-low. Has come to refer to any sexual activity conducted in secret. The fact that it shares its initials with the disabled list for professional athletes is purely coincidental.

DM: Direct Message. A fun option provided by your social-networking providers that allows the idiots you feel comfortable ignoring via email to harass you on an entirely new and even more intrusive platform.

DNR: A Do Not Resuscitate order. One of the most difficult decisions anyone whose beloved family member has been hooked to tubes and communicating through sucking noises for the last eight months will ever be so unbelievably overjoyed to make.

DOABLE: Easily accomplished by delegating to an idiot.

DOCTOR:

A PERSON WHO GOES THROUGH ROUGHLY FOURTEEN YEARS OF TRAINING TO BE LICENSED TO GIVE YOU TWO AND A HALF MINUTES OF MOSTLY PREOCCUPIED ATTENTION PER VISIT.

DOCUMENTARY:

A movie about real people experiencing something that really happened. *Way* too much reality for idiots.

DOG:

A CREATURE THAT IDIOTS CONVINCE THEMSELVES LOVES THEM MORE THAN ANY OTHER HUMAN, WHEN IN FACT SAID CREATURE WOULD SELL THEM UP THE RIVER FOR WHOEVER OFFERS THEM THE NEXT SLICE OF BREAD.

DOG PARK: Recreational area for canines, all of whom wish they had the power of speech so they could tell their idiot owners that the person they are using their dog to hit on is simply not good enough for them.

DOG POOP: A substance left on the sidewalk by idiots, as a way of indicating the one thing in nature that most closely resembles their brains.

DOGGIE BAG: A term that obviously got started in a much more vibrant economy, when restaurant leftovers could be wasted on the family dog instead of being repurposed as tomorrow's lunch.

DOLPHIN: Majestic, highly intelligent marine mammal whose sole function is to help humans put another notch in our New Age belts by letting us swim with them and tell everyone how magical it was.

DONE: An exclamation meant to indicate that one is finally, irrevocably through with whatever frustrating condition one is putting up with. Roughly translated, the phrase actually means "I am most likely going to keep putting up with this frustrating situation."

DOOR: Often the only thing standing between you and the idiot who will eventually come through it.

DOORMAN: A small and rather hollow facet of your upscale building's attempt to make you feel like you will never get robbed.

DOORMAT: A person who lets people walk all over them. Rather a misnomer, since most people either ignore the doormat completely or simply give it a couple of perfunctory scuffles, as if that will prevent a day's worth of dirt, grime, and sidewalk bodily fluids from entering one's home.

DOWNSIZING: Not only an insultingly naive business buzzword that means you are getting the axe, but one that has not, to date, ever been mitigated by any future "upsizing."

DOXXING: The publishing of another person's private information on the Internet, usually with malicious intent. At last, the entire world is truly the walls of a public toilet.

DRAMA: Either a genre of movie or an idiot's behavior pattern of drawing everyone into a nightmare of histrionic overreacting. Sadly, it takes us far too long to learn that both can be walked out on if we so desire.

DR. SEUSS: In our lives let's not get all funtzin or drumble; it's a shame if each day we act spingy or bumble—for old Dr. Seuss knew the happiest plonkers are people who talk like they're batsh*t bonkers!

DRAGON: Fire-breathing, winged reptile. But enough about your mother-in-law.

DREAM BIG: A naively precious phrase that assumes everyone has the same access to lofty ambitions. Whoever came up with Dream Big should be punched big.

DREAM CATCHER: Sacred Native American object turned into the equivalent of fuzzy dice.

DREAMS: Things you have the power to make come true simply by walking through the halls of your old junior high school in nothing but your underwear.

DRILL DOWN: A way of saying that you want to dig deeper into a given problem that also makes the entire conference room picture you having rather comical sex.

DRIVE TIME: Morning and evening segments of the day in which a trio of giggling, hyena-like disc jockeys fill our commutes with a symphony of overlapping forced laughter. Or you could just pop in an audiobook.

DRIVER: The person in movies who somehow feels entirely comfortable taking their eyes off the road to look at their passenger for, like, three minutes at a time as the audience waits breathlessly for a collision that never comes.

DRIVER'S LICENSE: The wallet-sized item on which the photo of you looking like the biggest dork in the history of mankind is preserved in plastic for sometimes dozens of years.

DRIVING: An activity that turns previously compatible couples into snarling, judgmental idiots who can't believe you didn't a) brake sooner, b) pass that idiot, or c) refrain from driving headlong into an abutment as a way to cope with my constant badgering.

DRONE: Since this unmanned aerial device is used to both drop bombs in war zones *and* drop a package off at your front door, it is only a matter of time before the war zones start getting the Amazon® deliveries and the front doors get the bombs.

DRUGS:

A SCOURGE ON OUR SOCIETY, DRUGS DESTROY LIVES AND TEAR FAMILIES APART. OF COURSE, SO DO A BUNCH OF OTHER THINGS, BUT THEY DON'T HAVE TONS OF TAXPAYER MONEY AND BADASS GOVERNMENT OPERATIVES WITH AWESOME BATTERING RAMS AND NIGHT-VISION GOGGLES COMING AFTER THEM.

DRUNK DRIVING: Irresponsible, endangering behavior that might be acceptable if we could guarantee that only the irresponsible, endangering idiot would be the one to buy the farm.

DUCK FACE: The last refuge of an idiot.

DUDE: Synonym for a guy that originated in surfer culture and has evolved into a unisex term for anybody you are addressing or referring to for any reason, ever and I certainly hope you surfer dudes are happy because this damn thing is not going away anytime soon.

DUMPSTER DIVING: Scouring through a bunch of trash hoping to find something useful. Sound familiar, ladies?

DVR: The 21st-century digital version of the shelf containing all the books you will never get around to reading.

DYING: Your only real chance to stick it to your creditors.

DYLAN, BOB: Winner of the Nobel Prize for Mumbling.

DYSFUNCTIONAL: A word we use to make light of having been raised by unrepentant troglodytes.

E-BOOK: Literature consumed in electronic form on a screen. And if you are reading this book on a device, remember that the larger you make the font, the funnier it gets.

E-COMMERCE: A way to make your entire persona vulnerable to attack. And more than bloody worth it for the convenience of never having to get off your ass and go to a store.

EARBUDS: Handy tool for communicating to those around you that you have no intention of communicating.

EARLY TO BED AND EARLY TO RISE: Makes a man early to bed and early to rise. At least as far as we can tell.

EARS: Forget eyes. In the 21st century, these are really the things we can't believe.

EARTH: A PLANET THAT WILL DO JUST FINE AFTER HUMAN BEINGS FINALLY BRING THEIR OWN SORRY SPECIES TO A VIOLENT END ON IT NEXT WEEK.

EARTH DAY: Annual commemoration in which we tell the planet that we're sorry, and that we're looking into other places to go once we've used her up like a cheap whore.

EASY LISTENING: Like spreading mayonnaise on music.

ECONOMY, THE: What all of our public officials campaign on, as if they think we're idiots who don't understand that all they are doing is moving the imaginary money around to make sure their cronies never have to worry about health care.

ED (ERECTILE DYSFUNCTION): As if that's the only thing dysfunctional on a guy.

EDISON, THOMAS: Inventor of electric light and the phonograph, and holder of the patent on the Let's-Make-Nikola-Tesla-Disappear machine.

EDUCATION:
THE GAINING OF KNOWLEDGE ESSENTIAL TO REMAINING ENLIGHTENED AND COMPETITIVE IN THE MODERN WORLD. LAST RECORDED EXAMPLE OF THIS OCCURRING: UNKNOWN.

EDUTAINMENT: Entertainment and education combined. And the reason your child's hopelessly analog third-grade teacher is no longer relevant.

EFFORT: Not worth the effort.

EGGS: What you've been putting in one basket this whole time, admit it.

EGO: This inflated sense of self-worth and importance is a crucial component in achieving positions of power in various business endeavors and in public office. Hence, people who have a healthy sense of who they are and therefore would never seek power or public office end up being ruled over by a bunch of dangerously unstable nut balls. Kind of beautiful, really.

EINSTEIN, ALBERT: Still, after all these years, an icon who remains the only available shorthand for a smart person. Kind of sad, really.

ELEVATOR PITCH: The quick, punchy sell of your most employable qualities, which you are encouraged to have memorized should you ever meet an influential person in an elevator. Do try not to take it personally when the aforementioned influential person keeps obsessively jabbing at the floor button while you prattle on like a desperate, unemployable idiot.

ELF: The little guy who is given the thankless task of trying to keep the mall Santa Claus sober.

ELVIS: The King of Rock 'n' Roll. Also the King of Barbiturates, the King of Thinly Veiled Deep Unhappiness, and the King of The Dark Side of Celebrity. But mostly the King of Rock 'n' Roll. Who is still alive.

EMERGENCY ROOM: Perhaps the very definition of irony, the ER is the place you would pretty much rather die than visit.

EMOJIS: An Internet-friendly way to express a wide range of emotions, including poop. And the fact that these annoying little visages have launched a movie franchise tells you all you need to know about Hollywood being out of ideas.

EMPATHY: The touching ability to hope you never have to go through the hideous crap your friend is going through.

EMPLOYEE: One who works for wages. Perhaps the most far-reaching definition of idiocy ever practiced by an overwhelming percentage of people who are otherwise idiocy-free.

EMMY: Since the advent of pay cable and streaming services, the Emmy is a television industry award given to those programs whose high level of sophistication is demonstrated by super-intelligent f-bombs and copious nudity.

ENERGY BARS: Imitation health food for people who think a lumpy candy bar is for some reason not a candy bar.

ENERGY DRINKS: Beverages that really keep you going. To the hospital.

ENERGY SUCK: Term for a person or activity that drains one's physical and mental resources. Just ask any idiot who gets married. And when you're through, ask any idiot who has kids.

ENTITLEMENT: The notion that one inherently deserves special treatment. Such a troubling and irritating epidemic among young people that their parents have had no choice but to enable it.

ENTREPRENEUR: A term that attempts to graft an air of dignity onto marketing your services as a clutter-reducer on Craigslist.

EQUAL: A state of being identical or equivalent, and a state into which we are all born, according to the U.S. Constitution. Of course, the U.S. has also produced a lot of great comedians.

EROTIC: In a world where one's requirements for sexual stimulation can run the gamut from a simple sheer negligee to getting turned on by bare-feet-crunching cockroaches, this word is truly an idiot's delight.

ETHICS: Ha-ha. LOL.

EVIL: A sickening, malevolent force, as found in serial killers and relatives who keep you on the phone for an hour.

EVITE: What happened when people realized that a simple group email lacks the crucial component of barraging your friends with ads.

EVOLUTION:

PROBABLY NEVER HAPPENED, OTHERWISE HOW COULD HUMAN BEINGS CO-EXIST WITH DINOSAURS, WHICH THEY OBVIOUSLY DID.

EVOO: Extra Virgin Olive Oil. An acronym invented solely so that foodies could sound street.

EXCLAMATION POINT: Punctuation mark that allows you to add a convenient "just kidding!" to the end of any email in which you have just ripped your co-worker a new one.

EXISTENCE: The state of being alive as defined by objective reality. And since objective reality is defined through video, it can be assumed that if you have not appeared on a reality TV show or had your dashcam shenanigans go viral, you don't exist.

EYES: The windows to the soul. But stop staring. There's nothing there anymore.

FACE: Once a set of characteristics that were with you for the whole of your wonderful, big life. Now, a set of easily manipulated characteristics that will end up giving your skin a frightening, stretched-out, mask-like appearance for the remainder of your sorry little life.

FACEBOOK: Social-media giant that has forced us into sharing the excruciating minutiae of our daily lives, on the Internet, with all the people we will never see again thanks to the Internet.

FACEPALM: Depending upon how many idiots you are forced to deal with every 24 hours, this wordless, hand-on-head expression of dismay could well occur more times a day than you have to pee.

FACIAL RECOGNITION SOFTWARE: Remember that protest march you unwillingly attended with your significant other? Well, you're screwed now.

FACT: An irrefutable truth that forms the basis for all deductive reasoning. Sadly, the facts that we're born, we live, and we die are pretty much the only irrefutable truths left, and even then somebody on the Internet is probably devising a way to say we're mistaken.

FAERIES: Tiny, winged beings in the ether that coexist with us and have magical powers to guide us on our way. And if you believe that, then your brains are made of gossamer.

FAILURE: Failure is nothing more than another chance to get things right. Actually, failure is failure, but you can't raise money for public television by telling the damn truth.

FAKE NEWS: Not sure how this happened, but the people who originally created the fake news have successfully gotten everyone to believe that the real news is actually the fake news now. Oh, wait, we are sure how this happened. We're all idiots.

FALL: A rapid downward movement, defeat in battle or utter collapse. We should really start calling it "autumn" exclusively from now on.

FALSE FLAG: A covert operation in which activities are designed to deceive people into thinking that they were carried out by a nation other than the one who is actually carrying out the covert operation. Trying to make sense of this definition is exactly why these operations work so well.

FAMILY:

PEOPLE RELATED TO YOU BY THE VERY BLOOD THEY SO
ADROITLY SUCK FROM YOUR LIFE FORCE.

FANBOY:

A MALE OF THE SPECIES WHO IS OBSESSED WITH COMICS, SCIENCE FICTION, OR OTHER FORMS OF POP CULTURE. APPARENTLY HARMLESS, UNTIL ONE REALIZES THAT HIS ACTION FIGURES OUTNUMBER HIS FRIENDS. AND THAT IT WOULD ONLY TAKE TWO ACTION FIGURES FOR THAT TO HAPPEN.

FANTASY: Either an elaborate, often sensual scenario played out in the mind, or a genre of literature that features wizards, dragons, and mythical kingdoms. Both rather masturbatory in not-so-different ways.

FANTASY FOOTBALL: A way for sports fans to think they are engaged in a game of strategy, as opposed to a geekfest that is one rung down from a Renaissance Faire.

FAQS: The section of any given company's website in which you are urged to leave them the f*ck alone.

FARMING:

A NOBLE PROFESSION THAT CONNECTS ITS PRACTITIONERS WITH THE LAND AND ALLOWS THEM TO SUPPLY ENTIRE NATIONS WITH THE LIFE-GIVING FOOD NEEDED TO SURVIVE AS LONG AS THEY KEEP BUYING SEEDS THEY CAN NEVER REGROW FROM A BUNCH OF HEARTLESS CORPORATE DIRTBAGS.

FASHION: Trends in dress or behavior. Commonly established by dangerously toxic egomaniacs, paraded by dangerously unhealthy anorexics, and adopted by dangerously idiotic sycophants.

FAT: Either the condition of being overweight, or the actual substance that causes it. Problem is, we idiots can't really see it on the latter, and then it's always too late when it shows up as the former.

FATE: The force that does not close one door without giving you a window to jump out of.

FATHER: Either your male parent, or a priest. And if the latter is your former, contact the Vatican immediately.

FATHER'S DAY: A day set aside to honor the biggest tool in your life with a tool.

FAVORITE: The button on Twitter whose streamlined wording tracked more easily than "The Love I Never Got from My Parents" button.

FAWKES, GUY:

BRITISH REBEL WHO GAINED FOLK-HERO STATUS BY TRYING TO BLOW UP PARLIAMENT IN 1605; AND WHOSE ESTATE IS GETTING BUGGER-ALL FOR RESIDUALS ON THOSE *V FOR VENDETTA* MASKS.

FEBRUARY: The month that should be pronounced "Febrooairy" and no one ever tells you why it isn't.

FEELINGS: Annoying, inconvenient things that we pray will no longer be necessary once the cyborgs take over.

FEMINISM: The belief that women are entitled to equal rights. No, that's okay, idiots, we'll sit here and wait while you formulate your argument against that.

FIDGET SPINNER: A stress-relieving tool originally designed for children with learning disabilities that became an intelligence-relieving tool for people with life disabilities. Also something that will have been forgotten about by the time you read this.

FINGER POINTING: Always remember: when you point a finger at someone, you also have three fingers that are sort of, like, curled up in a partial fist position and are, if anything, pointed at the lower part of the palm of your hand and not really pointing back at you at all, at least in any kind of convincing, literal way. So there's another idiot maxim out of the way.

FIREWORKS: As bloated examples of overcompensating for unexamined inadequacies go, this is right up there with the penis-extension sports car.

FIRST WORLD PROBLEMS: Hilarious term thought up by privileged people who need a good laugh about the contrast between the indignity of a waiter bringing them the wrong dressing for their salads while 800 million people lack access to clean water.

FISH: High-protein, low-fat food for people who don't mind a little latent radiation with their pilaf.

FIST BUMP: The handshake that says "You're probably still contagious."

FITBIT: Wearable technology that allows you to keep track of how many steps you took before you ran out of breath and died.

FIVE-HOLE: Soccer term used to indicate the space between the legs of a goaltender. Also used to indicate that footballers are either totally blind to double entendre, or take a perverse pleasure in supplying it to the world.

FLAG: A nation's emblem in cloth form, and something to wave around when you are fresh out of ideas.

FLASH MOB: A group of people coming together to perform something silly or poignant in public, capitalizing on the fact that it is totally in the moment, over in an instant, and never to be recaptured. Except by the incredibly spontaneous videographer they bring along with them to make sure that the agonizingly ephemeral event will live forever on YouTube.

FLEA MARKET: A yard sale in a trailer park.

FLESH: The outer coating of the human body that is, as Shakespeare said in Hamlet's famous soliloquy, heir to a thousand natural shocks. But none so naturally shocking as when it is on full display in a Walmart.

FLEX: In real estate, a term that refers to a home mortgage that generously allows flexibility in monthly payment requirements. Provides a wonderful opportunity for first-time homebuyers to plan for a future in any cardboard box on any street corner they could possibly want.

FLIP-FLOP: A term that lies dormant in the media for large periods of time until it is time for idiots to run for office again.

FLIPPING: Purchasing houses in order to make minimal improvements and then re-sell them at a substantial profit. It is probably just a coincidence that many practitioners of this activity take the same approach with their spouses.

FLOSSING: Or, as it is known in your house, *There Will Be Blood*.

FLOTUS: The First Lady of the United States, here made to sound like a toilet bowl cleaner.

FML: Acronym for *Eff My Life*. Most often used by people who have all their basic needs taken care of and cannot summon the perspective necessary to grasp that being overworked or going through a break-up is not quite the same as being a legless beggar in Calcutta.

FOLLOW YOUR BLISS: The concept of being guided by one's true calling, as attributed to the great teacher of mythology, Joseph Campbell. Possibly the most profound piece of advice ever given by a comfortably tenured college professor to a bunch of goofy, impressionable idealists who neglected to get a fall-back career.

FOMO: Acronym for *Fear of Missing Out*. Social-media–based anxiety aroused by the feeling that something exciting may be occurring without you. Used to cover up the painful truth that if something exciting is happening, it's probably *because* you aren't there.

FONTS: Something Microsoft® Word® long ago decided you should have eight hundred of, so that you could do a select-all on your bake-sale flyer and spend nine hours choosing the typeface that most conveys your kicky, off-the-wall sensibilities.

FOOD: Any of countless substances that provide nutrition, each with its own special booby trap of fat, cholesterol, sugar, or sodium waiting to go off and end you, no matter how damn healthfully you eat.

FOOD CHAIN: The hierarchy of organisms that hunt and kill one another for sustenance. And you wonder why the term is so often used to describe the chain of command at your workplace.

FOOD INSECURE: It's okay, they're not starving. They're just a little insecure. There, now you can get on with your lives and not feel so guilty.

FOOD NETWORK: All the excitement of watching on-camera personalities shove things into their mouths without having to pay extra for the premium porn channels.

FOOD PYRAMID: The U.S. Department of Agriculture's recommendations for proper consumption of the basic food groups. Laid out in pyramid form in order to inspire Americans to one day be healthy enough to build a structure weighing upward of 5 million tons using nothing but wet sand and a few lengths of very strong rope.

FOOD TRUCKS:

A HIPSTER-FUELED PHENOMENON THAT HAS SOMEHOW CONVINCED PEOPLE THAT A GRILLED CHEESE TASTES BETTER WHEN PREPARED AROUND TOXIC FUMES AND HANDED ACROSS A SALIVA-STAINED SIDEWALK FOR TWICE AS MUCH MONEY AS YOU'D LIKE TO PAY.

FOODIES:

POOR, DELUDED PEOPLE WHO NOT ONLY ACTUALLY THINK THERE IS SUCH A THING AS A GOURMET HAMBURGER, BUT ALSO POST PHOTOS OF IT ON SOCIAL MEDIA IN A PITIFUL ATTEMPT TO CONVINCE US THEY ARE ON TO SOMETHING.

FOOTBALL: 1. American sport known for its brain injuries. 2. European sport known for its hooligans. 3. Either way, somebody is getting their head smashed in.

FOREST: Serene, verdant natural space whose soft earth and canopy of trees provide the ideal place for contemplation of how it would be perfect for a kegger.

FRANCHISE: Either a corporate retail establishment made available for laypeople to own and operate, or a series of books or movies revolving around a recurring set of characters that are released in stages to maximize box-office grosses. Both strangely dependent on the public's tolerance for recycled garbage that insults one's intelligence.

FRAT: The building on a college campus that houses all the young men who engage in increasingly perverted ritual humiliations to work through their denial about their romantic feelings toward each other.

FREEDOM: The right to act as one desires, without the threat of hindrance or restraint. Oh, Christ, did we screw this one up.

FREEDOM OF SPEECH: See previous entry, add words.

FREUD, SIGMUND: The founder of psychoanalysis, and therefore most likely the originator of charging an hourly rate for only 45 damn minutes.

FRIDAY: Your weekly stay of execution.

FRIENDS: People that were real before Facebook.

FROYO®: A diminutive frozen yogurt, used in an attempt to graft an air of kicky coolness onto a product with less edge than a church social.

FRUIT: The stuff we always wash before eating, firm in our idiotic belief that six months of chemicals seeping into a pear can be magically removed by a run under our probably equally toxic tap water.

FUNNY: What that one idiot at work thinks he is. Are you going to tell him? I'm not going to tell him.

FUTURE, THE: A time still to come. And if the movies set in it are any indication, we simply can't wait to be going to war for water, choking to death in smog-choked urban blight, and fighting off pathologically violent throwbacks with an inexplicable attraction to scrap-metal masks.

GALILEO GALILEI: 17th-century Italian astronomer whose views about the Earth revolving around the sun found him branded a heretic and condemned to spend over 20 years of his life under house arrest. Damn, no wonder it's so hard for those people who hassle you outside the grocery store to get new issues on the ballot.

GAME CHANGER: Sports metaphor implying that an event has occurred in one's life or business that could potentially alter the way things proceed from that point on. So, like getting diagnosed with a terminal disease or dumping cable and getting a Roku.

GAME OF THRONES: *The Sopranos* with mud.

GAME ON!: Whatever, dude. It's just a group email about the office toy drive.

GATES, BILL: Co-founder of Microsoft®. Very wealthy philanthropist. Definitely not an idiot. Still doesn't make Excel any easier to work with. Just sayin'.

GAYDAR: One's reputed ability to sense whether or not a person is homosexual. It would be far more useful to be able to sense whether or not a person is a homophobe, a racist, or an all-around a-hole, but we idiots take what we can get.

GEEK OUT: To get all excited about an esoteric topic, such as why you haven't gotten any hits on your online dating profile.

GENDER FLUIDITY: A concept that's the bane of idiots whose worlds apparently revolve around controlling which bathroom people use.

GET OVER IT: Glib phrase meant to imply that one is unnecessarily hanging on to old emotional scars. And if you have ever had an idiot say this to you right in the middle of your depression or grief, you know that their death by strangulation at your hands is something you may also take a while to get over.

GHOST:
A LONG-DEAD PERSON WHOSE SPIRIT WAITS AROUND TO BE PLAYED BY A NON-UNION ACTOR IN A REENACTMENT ON A LOW-BUDGET BASIC CABLE SHOW.

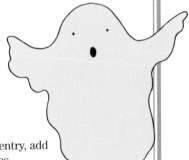

GHOST HUNTER: See previous entry, add pretentious night-vision goggles.

GHOSTING: In the dating world, ghosting is the noble practice of letting weeks of silence speak volumes about what a scumbag you are.

GIF: Graphic Interchange Format. File system that allows for elements of animation in an image. Without these, we'd never again experience rapidly repeating memes of Keanu Reaves.

GIFT: What each day is; that's why they call it the present. You idiot. I added that last part.

GIRL:

A YOUNG FEMALE; ALTHOUGH FULLY GROWN WOMEN ARE OFTEN REFERRED TO AS GIRLS, ALSO. BUT MOSTLY BY IDIOTS.

GLAMPING: Glamor camping. Wilderness adventure for people whose idea of roughing it ends at *Downton Abbey*.

GLASS HALF FULL: Some see the glass half full, some see the glass half empty. Some see a pathetic, overly simplistic metaphor for one's life outlook that has had a good run but needs to go away now.

GLASSES: Corrective lenses set into frames that have somehow come to confer an air of intelligence onto their wearers, when in fact they simply reflect the condition of myopia, or the circumstance caused by the focusing of light on one's eyes at the front of the retina instead of directly upon it. Come to think of it, you probably need to be smart enough to wear glasses to understand that.

GLUTEN: Proteins found in such grains as wheat and rye that help food keep its shape and could cause legitimate health concerns to less than 10 percent of the population; which doesn't stop the other 90 percent from being determined to freak out about whether or not everything they eat has gluten in it which, let's face it, it probably does.

GLUTEN-FREE: See previous entry, add driving waiters crazy.

GLOBAL WARMING: A phrase that unfortunately came into wide usage before the term "climate change," thus allowing idiots to claim that warming couldn't possibly be happening because, like, winter is still really cold and everything.

GOD:

A SINGLE, SUPREME, ALL-KNOWING, ALL-SEEING BEING THAT REPEATEDLY TAKES OUT INNOCENT PEOPLE JUST TO GIVE ATHEISTS A RATHER CONVINCING TALKING POINT.

GOLD: A metal whose only real value is that which we have assigned to it. So, it's really not so hard to understand how we once made somebody named Justin Bieber famous.

GOLF: Outdoor sporting event famously dubbed "a good walk ruined." But this is not really true, because it actually isn't even a good walk.

GOOGLE: A technological advance that has eliminated all cognitive reasoning in humans by removing their ability to recall the name of that one song or that one guy who was in that one movie with the power of their minds alone.

GOOGLE EARTH: While we're complaining about how intrusive it is that the Internet allows advertisers to track our buying habits, no one seems to give a crap that a serial killer sitting naked in his mother's basement can zoom in on our front door and maybe even figure out that's us in the still photo, wearing sweatpants and taking out the trash.

GOPRO®: Just what we need. A device to make us sit through selfies that move.

GOVERNMENT: Our local, state and national representatives, working tirelessly on our behalf to grease each other's palms and leave us out of the equation entirely.

GPS: The 21st century's way of assuring that you can no longer read a map to save your life.

GRADES: Letter-coded assessments of one's performance in school. One should always strive to achieve a C or a B grade, since you want to be perceived as just enough of an idiot to still be cool.

GRAMMAR: A concept so irrelevant to an increasingly image-based culture that it is about as dead as print itself. (Thank you for buying this book and helping us hold off the death throes.)

GRAPEVINE: The place through which bold-faced lies circulate for us to enjoy sharing them with others.

GRAPHIC NOVEL: A novel in the sense that it bears no resemblance to a novel at all.

GRAVITY: Either the force that makes our bodies sag as we get older, or a rather scientifically inaccurate movie starring Sandra Bullock. The first is a troubling precursor to our demise, yet the second is somehow more irritating.

GREATNESS: Of great eminence or high standing. Some are born great, some achieve greatness, and some have greatness thrust upon them. Still others are just really good at thrusting, which has been about the best we can do for greatness lately.

GREED: At last, something Democrats and Republicans can agree on.

GREEN: All-purpose term denoting lifestyle choices that favor the environment. Extremely comforting to those who think that bringing their own mug to Starbucks is going to single-handedly save the planet.

GREETER: Person planted at the entrance to a retail establishment to make customers feel that much better about where their lives have gone.

GROUNDHOG DAY: A movie about a man who is cursed to live the same day over and over. So, yes, it's a documentary.

GROUPIE: A person who gets a thrill out of sleeping with a superficial narcissist who will forget them instantly. Perhaps in preparation for the superficial narcissist who will forget them instantly whom they will one day spend the rest of their life with.

GUARDIAN: The person other than your accompanying parent that you hope will be with you when you want to get into an R-rated movie.

GUILT: That terrible feeling that overcomes you when you have done something completely unconscionable and realize you were this freaking close to getting away with it.

GUM: A product created to make up for a human being's shocking lack of a cud.

GYM: The place where you pay money to use machines that duplicate stuff you could be doing outside for free.

HACKER: Sort of your pain-in-the-ass, antisocial adolescent child, but with the ability to bring about the end of the world.

HAIR:

1. AN OUTGROWTH ON THE HUMAN HEAD THAT WE STILL, EVEN AFTER ALL THESE YEARS, BELIEVE CAN BE MADE SEXIER BY USING SOMETHING CALLED "CONDITIONER."
2. STUFF THAT WAS PUT THROUGH SO MANY HUMILIATING VARIATIONS DURING THE 1980S THAT IT'S A WONDER THE ENTIRE POPULATION HASN'T SIMPLY KEPT THEIR HEADS SHAVED SINCE THEN.

HAMBURGER: Fast-food item that has already included bacon, eggs, potato chips, and donuts among its toppings and clearly will not stop until it offers a human arm between its buns.

HAMILTON, ALEXANDER: American statesman, Founding Father, and founder of the *New York Post* newspaper, which was a rather shameless bid to make sure the Broadway musical based on his life would get a decent review.

HANDS:

SIMPLE APPENDAGES AT THE ENDS OF ONE'S ARMS WHICH, EVEN AS THEY LET HUMANS BUILD GREAT SKYSCRAPERS, COOK MOUTH-WATERING MEALS, OR PLAY A VIRTUOSO VIOLIN, WILL NEVER BRING AS MUCH GRATIFICATION AS THEY DO WHEN EXTENDING THEIR MIDDLE FINGERS TO SOMEONE WHO SO RICHLY DESERVES IT.

HAPPY: What we can all remember being in a time so long ago that we have forgotten we were most likely unhappy then, too.

HAPPY PLACE: An external location or state of mind that produces gushing feelings of great joy. All we ask is that you dial it back a little, because you're making us very uncomfortable.

HASHTAG: A way of letting social media users know the general idea behind your post, since the post itself obviously didn't convey it, you idiot.

HATE: A strong word to apply to someone you have never met who has carelessly taken up two parking spaces, but damned if it doesn't work just fine.

HATE SPEECH: Idiot speech.

HAVING IT ALL: Longtime ambition of so many people, and utterly attainable by simply exhibiting no human feeling, not caring about the needs of anyone but yourself, and either symbolically or literally murdering every clueless, weak-willed idiot who stands in your way. Go for it.

HAWKING, STEPHEN: Unbelievably intelligent person whose brilliance is all the more significant given the incredible physical obstacles with which he was beset. And yet, Eddie Redmayne wins the Oscar®. Go figure.

HEADLINES: Brief rundowns of daily news events that nobody reads beyond anyway, so you can take your two-sides-to-every-story and flush it down the toilet.

HEADPHONES: What you are wearing just before the 18-wheeler's air horn is the only thing louder than your playlist.

HEALTH: In one of the great examples of alcohol-related human idiocy, health is the thing we drink to.

HEALTH CARE: Where did you get the idea you were entitled to this? Just die already, will you? (U.S. only)

HEALTH FOOD: A plant-based, billion-dollar industry that is responsible for a subset of noxious farts that make the wind passed by a meat-eater seem like night-blooming jasmine.

HEART:

TO SOME, SIMPLY THE ORGAN THAT PUMPS THE BLOOD AND ALLOWS FOR OUR CONTINUED SURVIVAL. TO OTHERS, THE VERY MANIFESTATION OF LOVE, KINDNESS, AND HUMAN UNDERSTANDING. AND TO STILL OTHERS, THE PESKY PART OF THE EQUATION THAT MUST BE IGNORED WHEN EITHER EATING A CHEESEBURGER OR SCREWING SOMEONE OVER IN A REAL-ESTATE—OR EXTRAMARITAL—AFFAIR.

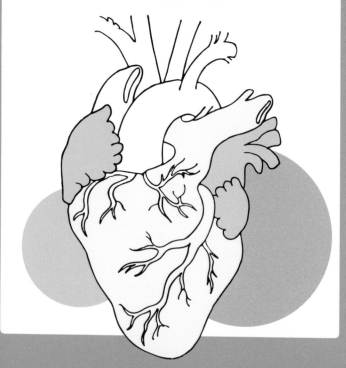

HEAVEN: The place where all your deceased loved ones are waiting for you to join them in order to play out whatever dysfunctional, co-dependent dynamic you had with them for all eternity.

HELICOPTER PARENT: An adult who cannot stop hovering over his or her child and micro-managing every aspect of their lives. These folks usually only back off when they are at a loss to understand how their kid got into drugs and prostitution.

HELL: As Jean Paul Sartre famously said, "Hell is other people." As other people have famously said, "Who the hell is Jean Paul Sartre?"

HELP: The section of a website's pull-down menu that offers its users invaluable assistance in killing an hour.

HENRY THE EIGHTH: A ruler who did whatever he wanted and operated solely on the basis of his own ego. Couldn't happen again, though, so we're good.

HERO: The person in the story who always prevails over incredible odds, providing an inspiring example of how we can be the hero in our own lives by not believing in this crap anymore.

HIGHWAY: Part of a mighty series of roads that connect your great nation, built by people who had a glorious vision of a world where ease of traveling great distances would destroy the unity of the family, decimate the natural landscape, and give us lung-choking pollution all at the same time.

HIKE: A long walk through nature, wherein three out of the six people dressed like Australians and subsisting on trail mix wish they had stayed home.

HIPSTER: A person who pointedly follows trends that are outside the cultural mainstream, little realizing that these are nonetheless still trends and therefore about as hip as a sitcom on the Disney Channel.

HISTORY: Apparently, something we are doomed to repeat even when we do remember it.

HIT: What a musician wants, what a YouTube video-maker needs, and what a hired assassin is able to monetize far more efficiently.

HIT MAN: Someone who kills people for a living. Unfortunately, nobody gets paid to kill dreams for a living, but that didn't stop your parents.

HOLD: The endless, sucking void of time in which you are placed every time you phone your cable provider for tech support.

HOLIDAYS, THE: God's way of forcing you to spend time with those idiots you normally keep safely in a frame on your desk.

HOLISTIC: An approach to medical science based in large part on shelling out eight weeks' pay on sixteen different bottles of herbal gel caps whose effectiveness is tenuous at best.

HOME DEPOT®: Building-supplies retailer whose clandestine installation of testosterone misters at every store entrance is only just now coming to light.

HOME OWNER: Sad, stressed-out zombie who dreams of the far more hassle-free cardboard box.

HOME THEATER: Gigantic, auditorium-worthy screen and sound system, most often installed by idiots in small apartments with neighbors above, below, and on the sides, all of whom go into an instant shudder of terror the moment the orchestral music that accompanies the movie studio intro kicks in.

HOMEWORK: Assignments that allow students to forget what they have just learned at home in the same way they forget what they have just learned in the classroom.

HORNY: All sexed up, and, if you are actually someone who still says the word horny aloud, probably with no place to go.

HORROR MOVIE: A stunning metaphor for life, in that the best approach to experiencing it is to show up, grab a friend for support, and try to get through it without having a heart attack or puking.

HOSPITAL: A PLACE OF HEALING. IF PAPERWORK CAN BE CLASSIFIED AS HEALING.

HOST: By one definition, the figurehead of a television news or entertainment program. By another definition, the entity that is the basis of origin for a deadly parasite. When you can tell the difference, let us know.

HOT: Word used to indicate a high temperature, an unusually attractive person, a topic that is either newly popular or could be considered off-limits, a state of agitation, spicy food, a branch of specialized knowledge, or someone who is difficult to deal with. Dear God, the only other word with that many different interpretations is God.

HOTEL: The place that charges you hundreds of dollars a night just for the privilege of having the first piece of toilet paper folded into an easy-start triangle for your convenience.

HOTEL CALIFORNIA: 1970s pop song that will never, ever, ever, ever not be played once a day, somewhere, for the next ten lifetimes.

HOT MESS: Term for someone who is really attractive but whose inherent dysfunction will probably drive you to ruin or perhaps even take your life. Line forms on the right, idiots.

HOTTIE: Base, superficial term for an attractive person that, when it is applied to you, has no right to be as flattering as it is.

HOURGLASS: The icon on your computer that sits there flipping up and down for minutes on end, just daring you to give in and do a restart. Mac users know it as the spinning beach ball of death.

HUGE: Once a word set aside to describe things that were truly enormous; now an overused bit of hyperbole used to explain one's feelings about a key play in a sporting event or discovering a two-elliptical gym in your new apartment building.

HUMANS: The only species that needs stuff besides food, water, and shelter in order to want to keep on living.

HUMBLEBRAG: To engage in false modesty, with the intention of getting others to notice something you are proud of. Yeah, um, so pretty much everything you've posted on social media since day one.

HUMILITY: A humble, realistic view of one's own importance in the scheme of things. Admirable, but no less tragic when you're the first to go during the coup.

HUNK: An attractive, muscular man, and someone for normal guys to hate the way normal women hate the *Sports Illustrated* Swimsuit Issue.

HUNGER GAMES, THE: Dystopian book and film series about a future in which we subject young people to a life-or-death competition and let everybody watch. Wait, this is the *future*?

HURT: Physical or emotional pain. The first is over quickly, the second can last a lifetime. Or at least as long as it takes for you to help pay off your therapist's mortgage.

HYBRID: The National Public Radio of cars.

HYPERBOLE: Exaggeration for effect. Sample usage: *claiming there are billions of idiots in the world is not hyperbole.*

HYPOTHESIS: A general theory proposed as an initial starting point to a larger conversation. For example, one could hypothesize that very few people know what a hypothesis is, and go from there.

I: Yourself. Or, what you need to get over if this relationship is going to continue.

I.C.E.: The Department of Immigration and Customs Enforcement. Sure, they might be preventing something terrible from happening, but you just know they're at least partly to blame for you having to take off your freaking shoes and put your freaking liquids in separate freaking plastic bags.

I COULD CARE LESS: No, you couldn't, actually, because saying you *could* care less implies that there are other levels of uncaring you may care to explore, which is incorrect, and which is why you should start saying "I Couldn't Care Less" immediately before you get slapped really hard.

ICEBREAKERS: Techniques for easing initial tensions between groups of people in order to begin a larger conversation. Or, as it is known in the field, making everyone's sphincter muscles clench with a deep and profound sense of awkwardness.

ICYMI: Acronym for *In Case You Missed It*. We shall wait patiently for *IABWGIMIWIIYI* (I Am Bloody Well Glad I Missed It, Whatever It Is, You Idiot) to take hold soon.

IDEATE: To think. Like we needed this word. Clearly invented by the same idiot who came up with *strategize*. Or *bigly*.

IDENTITY THEFT: What happens when some random idiot nonetheless manages to pull of something way smarter than you ever could.

IDEOLOGY: A collection of ideas that form the basis of a political system. As a rule, we idiots tend to keep swinging uneasily between Gandhi and Genghis Khan.

IDIOT: An ignoramus, a simpleton, a cretin, a moron, a dolt, an imbecile, a fool, a halfwit . . . stop me when I've described your boss, your spouse, your child, or yourself.

IGNORANCE: A state of unknowing and unawareness that, as the saying goes, is bliss. Well, if the 21st century is any indication, the entire world is so blissed-out on ignorance that it makes a million hippies on acid look like a toddler on a five-minute Slurpee® high.

IMHO: *In My Humble Opinion.* Usually the precursor to a statement that barely qualifies as an opinion and is about as humble as Kanye West.

IN YOUR FACE: Sometimes a statement about a creative endeavor that eschews subtlety, other times a taunt designed to upbraid a rival. The first is usually said *about* a douchebag; the second is usually said *by* one.

INCENTIVIZE: The idiot workplace equivalent of your parents promising you five bucks for a good report card.

INCOME: The substance that vanishes as soon as it appears, along with all the dignity you set aside to earn it.

INCOMPETENCE: A lack of ability to do anything successfully. Aside from our success at non-stop procreation, pretty much our legacy.

INCONSIDERATE: Heedlessly causing inconvenience to others. Now so commonplace in everyday life that our first reaction to someone actually being considerate is suspicion, and the firm belief that this idiot must be up to something.

INDIGENOUS: Not welcome here.

INDIGNANT: Anger at being treated unfairly. Or, as it is also known, anger at being alive.

INITIATIVE: Taking the opportunity to lead the way on something without being asked. Do not, under any circumstances, do this. No one will thank you, you will not be compensated financially, and your co-workers will start looking for ways to get you fired.

INSANITY: A term often defined as making the same mistake over and over while still expecting different results. Very bad news for anyone with a job.

INSTAGRAM: A constant, unrelenting source of photographic images so unnerving that it makes you long for the days when one packet of a dozen pictures took a week to get developed at the Fotomat®.

INSURANCE: A paranoia-based service that turns us all into idiots who always cave and go along with it . . . y'know, just in case we spontaneously combust or something.

INTEGRITY: The ethical part of us that cannot be bought. For less than a grand.

INTERNET ADS: Tiny, elaborately designed boxes that appear on your ISP's home page to offer you special prices on the last eighteen things you Google-searched barely .0000001 second ago.

INTERRUPTING: Something about as welcome during a conversation as it is during sex.

INVISIBLE: What you become the moment you arrive at a family gathering.

IPA: India Pale Ale. One of the more popular brews to capitalize on the concept of a "craft beer," a term used to trick idiots into thinking there could possibly be a more artistic way to make chilled urine.

IPHONE: Much like in Hollywood marriages, the old model is never around for long.

IRL: Acronym for *In Real Life*. Most of the people who use this abbreviation last encountered real life somewhere around the flip-phone era.

IRREGARDLESS: A word which was not a word until it got used so often by idiots that we just gave up and made it a word. Next thing you know, we'll just give up and all sorts of things that idiots do will become commonplace. Nah. Never happen.

ISLAND:

SOMETHING WHICH NO MAN IS, ACCORDING TO THE POET JOHN DONNE. OH, MR. DONNE, YOU COULD NOT HAVE FORESEEN THE INTERNET, WHICH HAS CREATED MILLIONS OF ISLANDS ON VIEW EVERY DAY, EACH ONE TRYING TO AVOID BEING RUN OVER WHILE THEY THUMB-JAB THE SCREENS ON THEIR DEVICES.

IT IS WHAT IT IS: A phrase used to convey playful resignation about the lousy movie you just wasted money on, or the lousy life you keep wasting breath on.

JANUARY: The start of a new year, and a time for a new resolve to improve one's life. Because nothing says "new beginning" like a thirty-below wind chill and it being already dark outside when you leave work.

JAWS: The movie that made us all learn to be terrified of blockbusters.

JAZZ: A genre of music that makes you feel like an idiot just because you don't know when you're supposed to clap for the stupid solos.

JEANS:

CLOTHING ITEMS ONCE DESIGNED FOR THE LIKES OF COWBOYS AND GOLD PROSPECTORS, ALL OF WHOM WOULD CRAP THEMSELVES TO DISCOVER THAT THRONGS OF IDIOTS ARE ACTUALLY PAYING EXTRA FOR THE ONES WITH RIPS IN THEM.

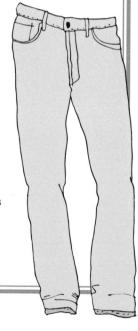

JESUS: When this dude finally comes back, he is going to make a fortune in intellectual property lawsuits.

JK: Acronym for *Just Kidding* that usually follows a tremendous diss and really means *Not Kidding*. NK.

JOB: That source of employment you idiotically said yes to some years ago, and through which you now grind as it leaves you feeling like an embittered, hollow husk at the end of each workday. But look on the bright side. You could be an embittered, hollow husk with the runs.

JOB INTERVIEW: An ever-evolving chance to lie about where you see yourself in the next five years.

JOBS, STEVE: Entrepreneur, inventor, co-founder of Apple. Did not live to see the release of the Apple Watch; probably would have died if he had.

JOHANSSON, SCARLETT: Popular box-office attraction who has appeared in many interesting and challenging independent film roles, none of which involve form-fitting superhero Spandex, so don't waste your money.

JOURNEY: Yes, a journey is a long, often spiritual excursion, but let's face it, it is really a 1970s band that has resulted in the world's largest-known quantity of karaoke larynx injuries.

JUDGE: A man or woman who holds the fate of many a litigant or criminal in his or her hands. Typically overloaded with cases and understandably in a hurry to motor through them. What a great recipe for justice.

JUICE BOX:

GAZILLIONS OF NON-RECYCLABLE, MIXED-USE CARDBOARD CARTONS AND INDIVIDUAL BENDY STRAWS CHOKING THE PLANET, ALL SO YOUR IDIOT CHILD CAN LET CUTESY PACKAGING PERSUADE HIM OR HER TO DRINK SOMETHING VAGUELY HEALTHFUL.

JUICE CLEANSE: A way to lose muscle mass and become emaciated while undermining your body's own natural ability to renew itself. No wonder you feel so healthy afterward.

JULY: The month in which American's celebrate their resolute independence and unwavering individuality by getting drunk and watching fireworks like everybody else.

JUMBOTRON: Giant screen at a sports stadium that happily uses your tacit permission to be videotaped in a public place to provide hours of profit-generating entertainment for which they do not have to pay you sh*t.

JUNE: The month that heralds both the beginning of summer and the ache in your soul that arises when you see backpacking college kids strutting through airports on their way to adventures in faraway lands while you negotiate screaming kids and a tightly wound spouse through baggage check on your way to Six Flags®.

JUNK FOOD: The nutritional equivalent of a cat-playing-the-piano video.

JUNK MAIL: When delivered to your physical mailbox, a minor irritation that will probably end up in recycling. When delivered to your online mailbox, a minor irritation that will probably end up making you hand over your life savings to a Nigerian.

JURY: Twelve people? Yes. Your peers? Not bloody likely.

JURY DUTY: The only obligation you will go to greater length to get out of than having to go see your friend's play.

JUSTICE: That deeply satisfying feeling of vindication you get when you realize how easy it is for rich people to avoid jail time.

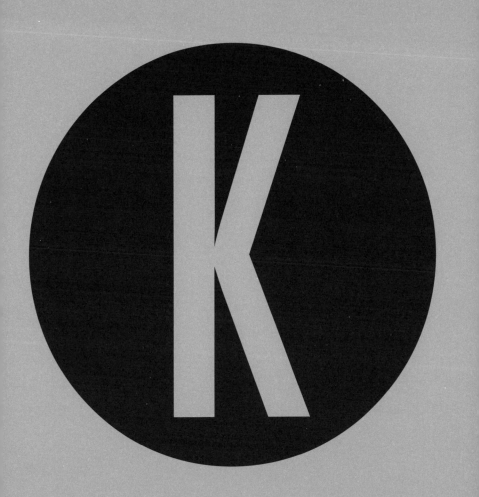

KALE: Cultivated plant from the cabbage family that languished in near-complete obscurity until suddenly appearing in every salad, protein shake, and bag of blue corn chips in the entire world. Clearly, the aliens want us healthy.

KARAOKE: The only form of public humiliation that supplies you with all the lyrics you need to hang yourself.

KARMA: The notion that one's behavior in this life can decide one's fate in future lives. Not to worry, since most of us die in this life, it's likely that the same fate will befall us in the next one, too.

KICKSTARTER:

DEPENDING ON HOW OFTEN YOU USE IT, A POTENTIALLY EXCELLENT WAY TO CHIP AWAY AT YOUR CORE GROUP OF FRIENDS, UNTIL THEY ARE SO FED UP WITH FUNDING YOUR HALF-ASSED SHORT FILMS, FANZINES, AND PRODUCT LAUNCHES THAT THEY DECIDE TO KICK-START YOU TO THE CURB.

KILL: Literally, to snuff out a life. Figuratively, to do exceedingly well at something—e.g., "You killed it, dude!" Only the black, black heart of the human race could come up with the idea of linking achievement with murder. They really killed it with that one.

KINDERGARTEN: College prep.

KINDNESS: Warmth or concern shown toward others. As you walk about your streets each day, you may never know how many people you touched through the simple act of being kind. Of course, most of them were off their meds and muttering incoherently to themselves, so they probably will never know it, either.

KITTEN: A little creature that restores one's faith in the gentler side of human idiocy, if only because it probably gets a trillion more hits on YouTube than the guys taking headers on their skateboards.

KNEE:

MUCH LIKE THE EMPLOYEES AT YOUR COMPANY, THE KNEE IS A PART OF THE BODY THAT HAS BECOME VERY EASY TO REPLACE.

KNOWLEDGE:

COMPREHENSION AND SKILLS ACQUIRED THROUGH EXPERIENCE AND EDUCATION. OR, AS IT IS KNOWN IN THE 21ST CENTURY, WATCHING *TMZ*.

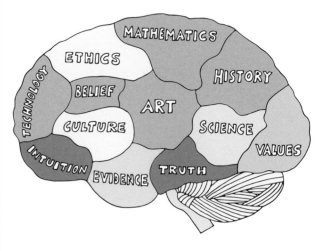

KUDOS: A by now meaningless expression of praise that is tossed about so freely it could apply equally to a getting a job promotion or getting pregnant.

LADY GAGA: Proof that Madonna and David Bowie had a one-night stand.

LANGUAGE:

THE USE OF WORDS TO COMMUNICATE. HONESTLY, I DON'T KNOW WHY I BOTHER.

LAP: The area of your body that you are doomed to keep completely still for three hours whenever a cat jumps onto it.

LAP DANCE: Like most things in life, an event whose inherent demeaning awkwardness can be handily undercut by cash outlay and liquor.

LASIK: Groundbreaking procedure targeting those who have worn glasses for so long that they want someone to slice up their eye pretty much out of spite.

LATE: Something idiots always have a sorry excuse for being; something pregnancy tests always have a positive way of confirming.

LAUGHTER: The healing, restorative outburst of joy that gets louder and more tragically forced and desperate in proportion to your consumption of alcohol.

LAW OF ATTRACTION: The belief that one's dominant thought patterns will bring positive or negative circumstances into one's life. What a load of crap. Oh, sorry, I mean, that's so beautifully and irrefutably true. (I mean, why take chances?)

LAWYER:
POSSIBLY THE BUTT OF EVEN MORE JOKES THAN BLONDES. AND, INTERESTINGLY, THE UNFAIRLY DEMEANING STEREOTYPICAL VERSION OF BOTH OF THEM WILL BE MORE THAN HAPPY TO SCREW YOU.

LEAD, FOLLOW, OR GET OUT OF THE WAY:
Empowering motto that teaches us to lead, follow, or get out of the way of arrogant pricks who say things like lead, follow, or get out of the way.

LEADERSHIP: The ability to somehow be paid six times more for being ten times less qualified.

LEAF BLOWER: Well, yeah, because everyone knows it's way more efficient to blow leaves out of the way than it is to collect and dispose of them.

LEGGINGS: Tight-fitting stretch pants that should come with a tag offering a gentle reminder about the fact that only about six people can get away with wearing them.

LEMMING:

A PERSON WHO UNTHINKINGLY GOES ALONG WITH A MASS MOVEMENT, NAMED AFTER THE SMALL FURRY RODENTS WHO WILL REPORTEDLY FOLLOW EACH OTHER OFF THE EDGE OF A CLIFF. WE SHOULD BE SO LUCKY THAT A SELECT FEW OF THEIR HUMAN COUNTERPARTS WOULD BE INCLINED TO DO THE SAME.

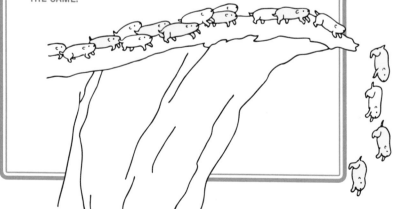

LEMONADE: What idiots always urge us to make when life gives us lemons. As if consuming our unceasing run of appallingly vile luck in liquid form will make it any more palatable.

LETTER:
APPARENTLY SOME FORM OF INFORMATION SHARING THAT OCCURRED BACK WHEN PEOPLE COULD ACTUALLY READ AND WRITE AT THE SAME TIME.

LIBERAL: People whose passion for their broad-based view of how the world should work is completely dwarfed by the passionate hatred they feel for those who don't see it that way. (*See also: Conservative.*)

LIBRARY: An institution that has somehow endured—free computers—in an age when books are obsolete—free computers—and information literacy is at an all-time—free computers—low.

LIBTARD: Derogatory term for anyone who thinks homeless people should not be euthanized.

LIE: As a noun, this word indicates a falsehood. As a verb, it indicates assuming a horizontal position. Interestingly, the latter is the position we assume to prepare for another round of the former each and every day.

LIFE: All the stuff that happens before you die. And don't be an idiot and start thinking there's anything else to it.

LIFE COACH: "Life is a crapshoot." Boom. You're a life coach.

LIFEHACK: Improving your time-management skills by finding new ways to interact with the devices that already consume far too much of your time.

LIKE: Once simply a designation of any particular thing or situation that brought about enjoyment. Now, a clickable social-media icon whose frequency and quantity represent your very worth (or lack thereof, you loser who only got two likes on that post) as a human being.

LINCOLN, ABRAHAM: 16th President of the United States, famously dubbed "The Rail Splitter," because he quickly left his folksy farm roots behind but continued to use them to help solidify his political image, and "Honest Abe" because he *never* manipulated the truth.

LINE: 1. A queue of people waiting to get into something. 2. Any given sentence or series of sentences in a literary or other work. 3. A glib phrase used in an attempt to seduce a person. 4. A measure of a dosage of cocaine. 5. When 4 is involved, 1 will be aggressively cut into, 2 will be either misquoted or repeated in an endless, twitchy fashion, and 3 will be botched completely. 6. Made you work for that one, didn't we?

LIPS: Something that could always be made a little more full and plump with a nice dose of injectable dermal filler, don't you think, idiots?

LISTENING: Making an effort to take notice of what is being said. And here is where we acknowledge all the readers who are going "What? I didn't hear you." Nice one, you guys.

LISTICLE: In the Town of Journalism, the Listicle is the whorehouse.

LITERALLY: Exactly or precisely. Or, as used in conversation by idiots ("I literally died." "She was literally on another planet"), neither exact nor precise.

LITTER: Carelessly strewn garbage, granular substance used to absorb cat droppings, or a group of newborn baby animals. Sure, *you* try teaching English as a Second Language and see how long you spend on this one.

LIVE CHAT: Customer-service option on banking and tech websites that commonly takes eleven times longer than talking to someone. But at least you don't have to talk to someone.

LIVE TWEET: To post a running commentary on Twitter about an event, usually one that is broadcast on television. Yet another way to get everybody who already thinks like you to enjoy the thrill of agreeing with you.

LOBBYIST: One who represents powerful interests and works to push their inhuman agendas forward in the political process. Other than that, they're great guys.

LOGIC: A course of action decided against more often than the use of a condom.

LOL: Acronym for *Laughing Out Loud*. Now used with such idiotic frequency that it has probably ended up as the accidental response to a death announcement way more times than we care to know.

LONELINESS: Despair caused by lack of company. Of course, there is no such thing as loneliness if we can learn to become best friends with ourselves. It should be noted, however, that when becoming friends with oneself, crushing boredom remains a distinct possibility.

LOSER: An insensitive word that reduces a person to a state of consistently unproductive failure which he or she probably does not deserve. Here's hoping "success-challenged" takes hold soon.

LOTTERY: A way for an idiot to have a little hope for a better future by throwing away money he could save for the future on the ridiculous concept of hope.

LOUD: Something idiots who talk on their cell phones in public have made an agreement with God to be.

LOVE:

SORRY, BEATLES, BUT IT'S NOT ALL WE NEED. WE IDIOTS
HAVE SEEN TO THAT.

LUCK: What we are sh*t out of.

LUNCH: The far less expensive meal that you should always suggest your friend meet you for if there is even the slightest chance that the idiot won't treat you.

MADNESS: What there is a method to. Please, dear God, let there be a method to it. We're dying here.

MAGICIAN:

SOMEONE WHO APPEARS TO HAVE INFLUENCE OVER OBJECTS OR CIRCUMSTANCES WITH THE USE OF SEEMINGLY SUPERNATURAL ABILITIES. THE FACT THAT YOU CAN'T FIGURE OUT HOW THE SON OF A BITCH DID IT DOES NOT MAKE YOU ANY LESS OF AN IDIOT FOR FALLING FOR IT.

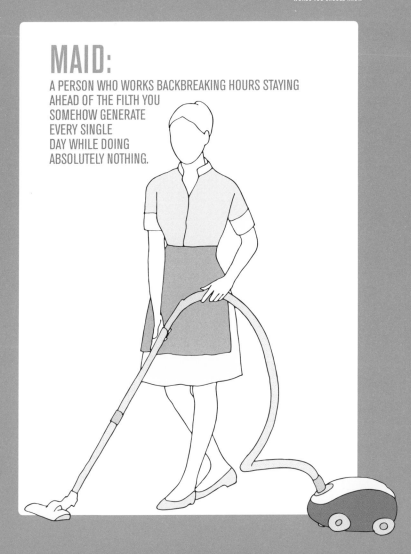

MAID:
A PERSON WHO WORKS BACKBREAKING HOURS STAYING AHEAD OF THE FILTH YOU SOMEHOW GENERATE EVERY SINGLE DAY WHILE DOING ABSOLUTELY NOTHING.

MAIN STREET: A haven of commerce and social interaction located across a short span of public roadway. Often romanticized as the nerve center of the charming American small town into which nobody different is allowed to set foot.

MAKE-UP SEX: Quick and intense release of whatever tensions had built up around a heated disagreement. Perfect for ignoring whatever tensions had built up around a heated disagreement and waiting for them to ultimately destroy your relationship.

MALL: A massive building containing everything you could possibly realize you actually don't need if you thought about it for even a second.

MAN: An idiot with a penis. If that's not redundant.

MAN CAVE: A room where the male of the species can go to take refuge from everybody who wishes he wasn't in the house anyway.

MAN HUG: A way men have of embracing one another that eschews lengthy bodily contact and is usually punctuated by two vigorous slaps on the shoulder blades. It's almost like men are such idiots about affection that they need to accompany it with at least some form of a punch.

MANAGEMENT: These are the idiots who always get the bump in position and salary because the idiots who hired them once got the same bump in position and salary. And it all goes back to the world's first job interview, in which the idiot doing the interviewing was suitably impressed by the resume of the idiot being interviewed because it listed "being an idiot" under special skills.

MANSPLAIN: An attempt by a male to make sense of his behavior, usually to a woman, and usually in a convoluted and often condescending way. This is exactly the type of idiotic nonsense that is only engaged in by 100 percent of the male population, yet somehow gives the entire gender a bad name.

MARCH: The third month of the year, traditionally noted for coming in like a lion and going out like a lamb. Although with the radical shift in weather patterns of recent years, March usually comes in like a seven-headed hydra and goes out like a *T. rex* on crack.

MARCH MADNESS: Term for the National College Athletic Association's annual basketball tournament. So named because of the madness that ensues when colleges allow their prestigious sports teams to pay dweebs to write their term papers.

MARIJUANA:

A SUBSTANCE THAT MAKES EVERYTHING AROUND YOU FUNNY. IF THAT IS NOT REASON ENOUGH FOR IT TO BE LEGAL EVERYWHERE, WE DON'T KNOW WHAT IS.

MARKETING: The process of identifying the selling points of a product or service that will seem most valuable to potential customers. Which is weird, because "brainwashing people into imagining they can erase all their inadequacies with a single purchase" has fewer words.

MARRIAGE: Perhaps the most sacred institution ever created for those who want to end up in an institution.

MARS: The next planet we plan to destroy.

MARVEL: A comic book brand that has taken over the world with its universe of superhero characters, paper-thin plots, and mandatory scenes of fictional U.S. presidents pounding their fists on conference room tables demanding action on whatever invasion of costumed bad guy weirdos is plaguing the world this time.

MASCULINE: A narrowly defined set of characteristics traditionally associated with the male gender that barely even touch upon the many different ways a man can express his inner nature. Although it's probably safe to say that if you are incapable of unfolding a beach chair, you may be denied admission.

MASTURBATION: A topic of discussion that had made no one a millionaire until Louis C.K. came along.

MATRIX, THE: Legendary sci-fi trilogy that posits a world in which machines use humans as an energy source while imprisoning them in a manufactured reality. Stop looking at your boss that way.

MAY: A glorious month of warmer temperatures in late spring, and the beginning of all the Internet ads for how you better damn well look like a fashion model in your swimsuit by summer or you will never get laid again.

MCDONALD'S®: Fast-food giant whose menu of largely fried and high-fat foods make them single-handedly responsible for the health problems of the millions of people who decide of their own free will to eat there.

MCMANSION: Donald Trump in hastily-constructed slab form.

MEANING: What human beings constantly search for, despite all evidence to the contrary.

MEDICATION: The stuff you pay hundreds of dollars a month for in order to survive—after too many years with the stuff you paid hundreds of dollars a night for in order to party.

MEDITATION: The practice of training the mind to tune out all judgment of one's thoughts and enter a quiet state where, after only a few precious moments, you begin to be aware of your own heartbeat and hence your own mortality—and then you freak out and call it a day.

MEGA: In metric units, the term denotes a factor of one million, but the prefix is now inserted before any number of words to imply an even more impressive status or quantity. Such as "megastar," used to denote a celebrity who will soon be in rehab to the factor of a million dollars.

MEH: Expression implying a shrug in response to something painfully mediocre. Uttered on more deathbeds than we'd care to note.

MELATONIN: Hormone generated by the pineal gland that can be taken in supplement form to combat insomnia. Go ahead and guzzle the stuff, but what's really keeping you up is replaying that fight you had with your ex and/or co-worker eight years ago and trying to work out just the right words you should have said to shut them down back then.

MEME: An aspect of pop culture that is duplicated on the Internet, often in the form of a photo with a humorous caption. Recent studies indicate that exactly three of them have actually been funny.

MEMORY: A brain function that conveniently gives out after extramarital affairs, wars, diets, and final exams.

MEMORIES: Happy recollections that we used to be able to draw upon within the limitless boundaries of our minds, but now can no longer summon without the aid of a jpeg.

MENSTRUATION: A word which some men believe will make them spontaneously combust if they hear a woman say more than three words about it. That it contains the word "men" conveniently does not register.

MENU, PHONE: The audio equivalent of an Escher painting.

MENU, RESTAURANT: Either a description of available food items written in flowery prose on the rarest vellum and promising much drizzle and frisson, or a plastic-coated collage featuring beauty-shot versions of dishes that will be far less plump and mouth-watering when they reach your table. The former is viewed by idiots who are paying way too much; the latter is viewed by idiots who have had too many children to pay way too much for anything ever again.

MEDIOCRE: That word you are searching for after most of your meals, movies, and sexual encounters.

METAPHOR: A description of an object or situation that cannot be applied literally, such as "this relationship is a noose around my neck." Okay, wait, bad example.

MEETUP: An informal gathering of losers with nothing better to do.

MICROAGGRESSION: A subtle, often thinly veiled form of discrimination that makes the recipient of it want to engage in some good old-fashioned macropummeling.

MICROCHIP TECHNOLOGY: A debit-card advancement that allows you to see your ATM card being declined in a remarkable, record-breaking 1/100,000,000th of a second.

MICROWAVE OVEN: Cooking device whose function has been affectionately called "nuking" for so long that we have rather submerged our fears over how many baked potatoes we'd have to eat before growing a third nostril.

MILK OF HUMAN KINDNESS, THE: A symbolic dairy product that measures compassionate behavior between humans, and is fortunately also available in reduced 2% form.

MILLENNIALS: Entitled young people whose self-assuredness about the world being their oyster is somewhat offset by the fact that they need to call their parents for help with changing a light bulb.

MINDFULNESS: A practice involving the peaceful acceptance of how things are and allowing the present moment to simply be. Lasts about as long as it takes for a nearby car alarm to go off.

MINIMALISM: A lifestyle choice in which material objects are eschewed and day-to-day life becomes simple and less encumbered. So, being down to nothing but a flat screen and Netflix would probably count, right? Right? Hello?

MINISTER: A man or woman of the clergy, to whom a community turns when they need just the right amount of soothing words to put them to sleep of a Sunday morning.

MISOGYNY: An ingrained prejudice against women. In deference to those who exhibit this prejudice, it's important to note that it can be brought about by any number of factors, such as being an idiot, being a douchebag, or being a moron.

MIXED MARTIAL ARTS (MMA):
WHAT HAPPENED WHEN BOXING WAS DEEMED A FAR LESS EFFECTIVE WAY TO BEAT THE LIVING SH*T OUT OF EACH OTHER.

MIXED SIGNALS: What idiots who wouldn't know a real human emotion from a tube sock always claim the other person was giving them.

MIXED-USE PROPERTY: All the excitement of actually living in a real neighbor-hood without that neighborhood being real.

MONDAY: The weekly emotional equivalent of the bear attack scene from *The Revenant*.

MONETIZE: To find a way to earn revenue from one's ideas. Often a challenge when it comes to the Internet, where the best strategy for monetizing one's tragically esoteric blog or impossibly ultra-niche YouTube channel is to go out and get a freaking job.

MONEY: Something people are usually happier without. Well, in movies about the dignity of poor people, anyway.

MONKEYS: Mammals of the order of primates. It has been said that a million monkeys typing on a million keyboards would eventually produce the complete works of Shakespeare. That means they could probably crank out *Fifty Shades of Grey* in about eight minutes.

MONKEY MIND: The uncontrollable, restless chattering in which our brains engage each day. And a completely fixable condition, if only we can learn to be silent and cease the habitual thought patterns I'll never make the rent this month and create a safe place for solitude nobody loves me and the tuning out of your dominating intellect I'll never be good enough for you, Dad. See, isn't that better?

MOON: The only natural satellite that permanently orbits earth. A majestic and awe-inspiring presence in the night sky that we idiots somehow turned into a slang term for showing our butt cheeks to each other—when Uranus was just sitting there waiting for its chance at that one.

MOTEL: The place where the one ice machine on every floor somehow manages to sound like it is right next to every room.

MOTHER:
SOMETHING EVERYONE HAS. MUCH LIKE OPINIONS AND BUTT-HOLES. DON'T TAKE THAT THE WRONG WAY OR ANYTHING, MOM.

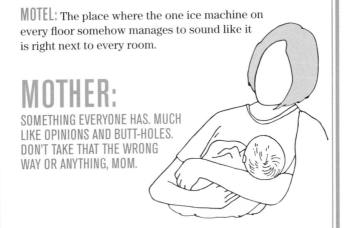

MOTHER'S DAY: Yet another example of how human beings set aside a single 24-hour period to commemorate something that should be honored all year.

MOTIVATION: The underlying reason for each action we take as humans. Or, as it is known to those who study our behavior: "push button get cookie."

MOTIVATIONAL SPEAKER: Someone to whom you pay thousands of dollars for the privilege of realizing that their path to success was their path to success and could never be duplicated by an idiot like you, no matter how much money give them.

MOTORCYCLE: God's way of saying that being at a higher risk for death is worth it if it means you can weave in and out of traffic jams.

MOTOR HOME: Domicile on wheels favored by folks who clearly never listened to the admonition "don't crap where you eat."

MOUNT RUSHMORE: Four giant heads carved into the side of a mountain. Only American tourists would think this was anything.

MOUTH: The one part of the human anatomy that could stop the idiocy as it makes its way from the brain, but sadly never chooses to do so.

MOVIE: Quaint old form of storytelling in which a narrative unfolds over two continuous hours. Died out shortly after the average commitment to the viewing experience failed to exceed eleven seconds.

MOZART, WOLFGANG AMADEUS: 18th-century composer and prodigy who wrote his first pieces of music at age 5. Which certainly makes one wonder why these idiot conductors need to be, like, 30, before they can do anything with them.

MUFFINS: Donuts for the deluded.

MUMBLECORE: Low-budget film subgenre in which characters in their 20s and 30s mostly talk about stuff and process their lives. Largely because they have finished college without any marketable skills and can't afford to do anything else.

MUSIC: The expression of the full range of mankind's complex array of emotions, which apparently consist entirely of the happiness that arises when meeting someone new or the sadness that arises when breaking up with them.

MUSICALS: It is time to put aside the superficial stereotype that enjoying musicals is somehow an indicator of someone who might be gay; when in fact musicals are merely an indicator of someone who seems to have no problem with people suddenly bursting into song for no apparent reason. And that kind of idiocy transcends sexual preference.

MUSK, ELON: Business magnate and inventor who has pioneered the Tesla automobile and space exploration, famously declaring that he would like to retire on Mars. Further proof that rich people will stop at nothing to get the hell away from the rest of us.

NAME: The words that denote who we are and where we come from. Neither of which we had any say in, and which give us all manner of stress-related diseases as we attempt to either make good on, outrun, or, in some extreme cases, deliberately defile them.

NANOSECOND: One billionth of a second. Figuratively, an extremely short amount of time. Literally, the amount of time it takes the idiot behind you to honk after the light turns green.

NARCISSISM: Exaggerated self-importance, insatiable need for approval, and a disregard for others' feelings. But it's okay, because the little bastards cannot stay eight years old forever.

NATION: Once a word which defined a group of people who share an entire geographical area and history, the term now seems to apply to any subset of nut balls who like the same baseball team.

NATIONALISM:

AN EXTREME FEELING OF PRIDE OF COUNTRY, OFTEN EXEMPLIFIED BY A SUPERIOR OR EXCLUSIONARY ATTITUDE TOWARD OTHER PLACES. AND WHY NOT? AFTER ALL, YOU'RE BETTER THAN THOSE OTHER IDIOTS, AREN'T YOU?

NATURE: What we are forced to take in when our phone battery dies.

NAUSEA: Feeling sick or queasy, possibly on the verge of throwing up. We can take heart in the fact that if we stop watching the news, we will never experience this feeling again.

NECESSITY: The mother of invention. As in, feeding your insatiable brood is a necessity, hence the invention of a soul-sucking day job. What a mother.

NECK PILLOW: A protuberance that idiots insist on keeping attached to their necks while walking around airports, seemingly unaware that they look exactly like the kind of idiots who wear neck pillows while walking around airports.

NEED TO KNOW: Whatever it is, when this phrase is trotted out, we idiots will never know it.

NEGATIVE: Realistic.

NEIGHBOR: The most noisy, inconsiderate a-hole that you will ever be reluctantly grateful for during an emergency.

NEPOTISM: The hiring of a friend or relative by those in a position of power or influence. Probably the ugliest, most resentment-inducing practice that you will ever hope happens to you.

NEST EGG: Money set aside upon which to build one's future and the future of one's family. Since whatever pittance you can save would likely not put even the smallest dent into a down payment or a year's college tuition, perhaps you could consider blowing it all on drugs or action figures.

NET NEUTRALITY: The concept that nothing on the Internet should be favored or blocked. Although uplifting videos about inter-species animal affection may have to go.

NETFLIX: Entertainment outlet whose vast collection of colorful jpeg posters creates a compulsion to click through thousands of pictures before finally being unable to decide on anything and ultimately going to bed. This precisely duplicates the hours of indecision spent in video stores in the 1980s and '90s, except then you had to travel back home in order to go to bed.

NETFLIX AND CHILL: Slang term for going back to one's domicile to have sex. We can only assume this was chosen unanimously over the far less sexy "Amazon Prime and Chill."

NETWORKING: Cultivating relationships with people you cannot stand in order to advance to a position you never really wanted.

NEW NORMAL, THE: What we call a once-unfamiliar set of unfavorable circumstances that have now become standard operating procedure. At work, this could mean anything from a reduction of benefits to a hiring freeze. In the larger society, it could mean anything from a new group of idiots running things to a new group of idiots running things.

NEWS: A whole lot of depressing stuff that we can do nothing about, which makes us feel powerless, which makes us feel angry, which makes us—and this is the really sick part—want to keep watching the news.

NEWSPAPER:

THE LAST BASTION OF IN-DEPTH REPORTING KNOWN TO MAN. UNFORTUNATELY, THE LAST PERSON WHO CARES ABOUT IN-DEPTH REPORTING JUST DIED.

NICE: A pleasant, agreeable quality that will get you absolutely nowhere.

NIGHTMARE: A dream that becomes highly unpleasant or terrifying. Capitalism?

NOVEMBER: The month in which the prospect of gathering together with family begins to loom close enough to make you Google "Xanax."

NSFW: Acronym denoting the phrase *Not Safe for Work*. Meant as a warning that the content of a forwarded email or video could offend the sensibilities of all the idiots in the world who cripple our economy by spending all day on the computer instead of bloody working.

NUANCE: Ironically, the remaining eight people who know what this word means are the same eight people who know that it doesn't exist anymore.

NURSE: The person at the hospital who probably knows more than the doctor but didn't want to take a career path that involved being an a-hole.

NUTRITION FACTS: The statistics on various vitamin, sugar, and fat contents printed on the labels of our store-bought food to alert us to any health risks. Yeah, and even if *people* came with these things, we wouldn't pay any attention to them, either.

OATMEAL:

A MUSHY SUBSTANCE PEOPLE CONSUME BECAUSE THEY HAVE HEARD IT CAN HELP REDUCE CHOLESTEROL. OF COURSE, THE REST OF THEIR CHOLESTEROL-LADEN DIET MAKES EATING OATMEAL RATHER LIKE TRYING TO MAKE UP FOR A WEEK OF FORNICATION BY GOING TO MASS ON SUNDAY.

OBLIVIOUS: Unaware or heedless of what is occurring around you. It is difficult to determine whether this state is more common among idiots in traffic, idiots walking around, or idiots in glaringly unhealthy relationships.

OBSTACLES: Those things in life that thwart us and break our spirits. But don't worry, it's like the famous wise old saying goes: if it doesn't kill you, it will make you wish you were dead.

OCEAN: Receptacle of surgical needles, human sweat and pee, nuclear fallout, six-pack rings, and, occasionally, fish.

OCTOBER: Transitional month bringing crisp air, leaves that change color and crunch underfoot, pumpkins, goblins, and, in retail outlets, the first freaking Christmas displays.

OEDIPUS: Character from Greek tragedy who discovered that he had murdered his father and slept with his mother. Dude would be laughed off of afternoon TV for not being controversial enough.

OFFENDED: Indignant over a perceived insult. Such as being told you are a humorless, easily offended little sh*t.

OFFICE:
A PLACE SO FILLED WITH HOPELESSNESS AND BROKEN
DREAMS THAT IT MIGHT AS WELL BE HOLLYWOOD.

OFF THE GRID: The state of being disconnected from the Internet and cellular communication. A condition we all dream of attaining, even as we know that not being able to check our email every twelve seconds would probably send us into anaphylactic shock.

OLD: Belonging to the past or being of advanced years. Basically, if you remember self-addressed, stamped envelopes, welcome to decrepitude.

OMELET: Something you apparently have to break some eggs to make. Damn, we idiots have made a crapload of omelets over the years.

OMFG: Acronym for *Oh My Effing God*. For those times when burning in hellfire for eternity seems a small price to pay for the impact of taking a simple OMG up a notch.

ON THE FENCE: Trying to decide where you stand as the brownshirts and tanks make their way toward your fence.

ONLINE DATING: Nothing more than the Internet-era version of a longstanding romantic tradition: beginning the courtship process on a foundation of lies.

ONLINE QUIZZES: A series of ultimately pointless exercises using a question-and-answer format to randomly determine which Disney villain you are most like or what your name would be if you were a Hobbit. Still waiting for the "Which Idiot Are You?" quiz, but we're not holding our breath.

OPERATION: What you definitely need and should have as soon as possible and don't ask any questions and it's for your own good and you'll be all better afterward and yes it's covered by insurance how else do you think I'm getting so rich?

OPINIONS: A point of view on any given subject, usually rooted in emotion, not fact. The general concession on opinions, therefore, is that they are about as welcome as a custom ringtone at a funeral.

OPPORTUNITIES: The right set of circumstances to bring about a favorable outcome. It is said that the key to life is being able to recognize when these opportunities present themselves. Sadly, the idiot who came up with this concept never took the leap into telling any of us how, exactly, to do this.

OPTIMIST: The one person who is still holding out for Adam Sandler's Oscar®.

OPTIONS: What we're fresh out of, thanks to the idiots.

ORANGE JUICE: Liquid refreshment that breakfast joints have no compunction about charging way too much for, while adding insult to injury by serving it in a glass the size of an Advil®.

ORDERS: What idiots always say they were following.

OSCARS, THE:
WHERE HUMILITY GOES TO DIE.

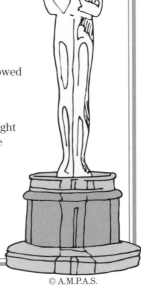

OSTRICH: Large flightless bird that would not be content until it was allowed to be a burger.

OTHER CHEEK, THE: What Jesus taught us to turn after being struck on one cheek, in a gesture of humility and pacifism. But go ahead and hit back. There are so many people taking huge liberties with the teachings of Jesus that this one can probably go.

© A.M.P.A.S.

OUTLET MALL: Several city blocks of name-brand merchandise, finally marked down to a price commensurate with the hourly pay of the sweatshop employees who make it.

OUTPLACEMENT: Helping people find jobs after firing them. Sort of like being given mouth-to-mouth by your murderer.

OUTSIDE THE BOX: A phrase indicating unconventional thinking. Commonly uttered by idiots whose idea of unconventional thinking ends at the concept of Casual Friday.

OVERSHARING: The revealing of an inappropriate amount of details regarding one's life. There is clearly no such thing as oversharing on social media, as anyone who has found the "my sister just lost her long battle with cancer" status update in their Facebook timeline will tell you.

OWNER'S MANUAL: The only document that is ignored more often than the Constitution.

OXYGEN: Colorless, odorless, tasteless gas that supports all life. Couldn't have described corporations better myself.

OXYMORON: The pairing of two contradictory words. Perhaps the most well-known example of this is "jumbo shrimp," but "altruistic cat" is also a good one.

PACIFISTS: People who get really angry when they think about the futility of violence, and even angrier when they realize they can't get their hands on enough weapons to take out all the violent people.

PAIN: What they say we must experience in order to grow, although there is a certain wisdom in the phrase *no pain, no pain.*

PANTS: What we idiots want to get into when someone else is wearing them. Then, what we want to get out of when the other idiot agrees to our request.

PAPER: The thing computers were supposed to save us from ever having to deal with again. That worked out well.

PAPER JAM: The copier function that has been left alone and walked away from more times than the victims of serial daters.

PARANOIA: Common sense.

PARENTS: Once revered and even feared figures of

authority, now enabling automatons so fearful of discord that they are incapable of overruling even the simplest demand made by a barely sentient toddler.

PARKING ATTENDANT: The only person in the world more inherently disinterested in you than your therapist.

PARKING STRUCTURE: An edifice that demonstrates mankind's inexplicable tendency to daily, and of its own free will, enter an enclosed space with hundreds of its most panicked, addled, and accident-prone fellow idiots.

PARTICIPATION TROPHY: A sweet way of encouraging our children to feel good about contributing virtually nothing to the fabric of existence.

PARTY: A raucous gathering attended by a host of desperate people who are hoping being raucous will make them forget the inadequacies that have made them so desperate.

PARTY, POLITICAL: An ideological affiliation adhered to by a host of desperate people who hope that having an ideological affiliation will make them forget the eroding conviction that has made them so desperate.

PASSIVE-AGGRESSIVE: Manipulation of a situation through indirect resistance to any suggested approach. This is the way idiots get things done. And God help the rest of us idiots, it works. Every time.

PASSIVE INCOME STREAM: A source of money that just keeps flowing in while you sit back and do nothing. About as easy to generate as the other type of stream, especially once you're over 50.

PASSWORD: A series of letters and numbers which allow you access to your ever-increasing list of online activities. FYI, you have by now gone through more passwords than you have gone through sex partners.

PATRIOTIC: Catch-all term used when swaggering around about the greatness of one's nation is the most convenient way to cover up that you cannot name a single article of the Bill of Rights, or, in many cases, spell the word "article."

PAYBACK: Something that is, at least according to most of the bad dialogue in action movies, a bitch.

PAY IT FORWARD: Being nice to someone other than the person who was nice to you. Sounds like a recipe for a face full of pepper spray, but knock yourself out.

PBS: Public Broadcasting System. Your home for a rich variety of non-traditional programming, from quaint British murder mysteries to quaint British murder mysteries.

PBS FUND DRIVE: That time of year when clip shows about dead musicians are used to solicit pledges from the people who will soon join them.

PEACE:
1. THE CESSATION OF ALL WAR AND VIOLENCE.
2. A STATE OF INNER TRANQUILITY.
3. BETTER GO FOR THE LATTER, BECAUSE THE FORMER AIN'T HAPPENING IN YOUR LIFETIME, FRIEND.

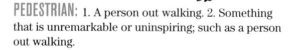

PEDESTRIAN: 1. A person out walking. 2. Something that is unremarkable or uninspiring; such as a person out walking.

PEN: What idiots never have when they need one, and what you are idiot enough to keep giving them, thus perpetuating a terrible cycle of pen codependency that will last from elementary school to college and beyond.

PENCIL: Obsolete writing implement that put its best years behind it and has resigned itself to being most useful as something to jam into someone's eye in a horror movie.

PEOPLE: The human beings that collectively make up society. Basically, there are two kinds of people in the world: those who set goals and spend every waking moment doing whatever it takes to meet them, and those who do not have a trust fund.

PERFECTION: A situation free of all flaws or downsides. Very difficult to attain, so one should not stress the mind and body by constantly striving to achieve it. However, striving to achieve perfection at not constantly striving to achieve perfection may well be worth the stress.

PERFECT STORM: Yet another victim of mankind's relentless need to make a positive out of a negative, this term is meant to describe a confluence of events that promise death and destruction, but now pretty much means any series of events that conspire to make an idiot rich.

PERFUME: Once his or her name is attached to it, perfume is the first indicator of a celebrity who either already is, or soon will be, a nonentity.

PERSONAL: Those things concerned with your private life and therefore kept to yourself. Unless you have a Facebook account, of course, at which point everything from a picture of the running sore on your inner thigh to that near miss involving autoerotic asphyxiation is fair game.

PERSONAL-SIZED: Smaller portions of everything from pizza to watermelon that some marketing genius came up with so you can feel like you are being catered to for being tragically alone.

PERSONAL SPACE: The highly coveted area around of each of us that we feel is psychologically our own, and which makes us uncomfortable when encroached upon. So the fact that we invented subways, theme parks, and raves is only further proof of our inherent idiocy.

PESSIMIST: Nothing more than a person who thinks eternal optimists are a pain in the ass.

PHARMACEUTICALS: Various compounds used to create medicinal drugs. Routinely used by a bunch of idiots who feel that the risk of vomiting, diarrhea, dry mouth, irritability, or death is more than worth it if they can have a chance to cure whatever condition they are not sure they even had in the first place.

PHOTOBOMB: To ruin another's photograph by inserting oneself into the frame as a prank. Given most of the useless photographs taken on people's camera phones at every second of every day, they could probably all use a little ruining.

PICK-UP TRUCK: Seriously, if you didn't want to be constantly asked to help people move, why did you even buy the stupid thing?

PICTURE: The thing that is worth a thousand words. Which is probably why words are going away, if you can picture that.

PIE: One of those things that idiots cite when espousing the idea that some foods are worth getting a heart attack for. Hey, even in the Dictionary of Idiocy, idiots are occasionally right about something.

PILATES:

MUSCLE-STRENGTHENING EXERCISE REGIME WHOSE PRINTED NAME RECALLS THE DUDE WHO GAVE UP JESUS TO BE CRUCIFIED. THINK I'LL GO WITH YOGA. AT LEAST THAT SOUNDS LIKE THE CUTE LITTLE JEDI FROM *STAR WARS*.

PIN: Personal Identification Number. 4-digit code used to access such services as online banking or your voicemail. Oh, yeah, 4 little digits. That's not hackable at all.

PING: To reach out to someone with a quick email or text message. Because in a technology-based age, we really do need ever-evolving terms for bugging the living crap out of someone.

PITT, BRAD: Handsome movie star who has taken on the much-needed role of making men feel inadequate for a change.

PIZZA:
A DELICIOUS FOOD PRODUCT THAT WAS DOING JUST FINE BEFORE SOME IDIOT DECIDED IT NEEDED ITS CRUST STUFFED.

PLAN: Forming a preset course of action, which, as they say, makes God laugh. Of course, then they also say that life is what happens while you're making other plans. But they also say Jesus is coming, so we should look busy. Time to find these "they" morons and tell them to get their stories straight so we can nail down the mother-fletching meaning of life already.

PLATO: Greek thinker and pivotal figure in the development of modern philosophy. His Allegory of the Cave attempts to show us that human beings are inextricably bound to the impressions of the world created by their own limited experience. Well, duh.

PLAUSIBLE DENIABILITY: The way senior officials in any given profession show the world that when the going gets tough, the tough get going on saying they were nowhere near where all the crap went down.

PLAY: A dramatic work that is performed on the stage and relies entirely on words to tell its story, without the benefit of hyperkinetic editing, slow-motion kickboxing, or car chases. I give it another year.

PLAY DATE: A way for parents to communicate to their children that fun is only fun when it is planned way in advance and doesn't last too long.

PLAYTIME: Engaging in silly games or foolish behavior purely for enjoyment. A freeing sensation so readily accessible as children, yet so difficult to tap into as adults. Perhaps because it is tough to make a game out of gradually realizing you aren't going to get anything you wanted and are sliding inexorably toward extinction. I mean, that's one theory.

PLEASE: Remember, kids: you should always use this word whenever you want something. Sometimes we forget, and that's okay. But, when addressing an idiot, you must never, ever, ever forget to include it before telling them to shut up.

PODCAST: Not sure how this happened, but there are now more podcasts than there are people.

POE, EDGAR ALLAN: 19th-century American pioneer of many literary genres and forms, yet constantly beset by financial hardship and substance-abuse issues. As skilled as Poe was at writing horror, he could never pen a tale as macabre as the one about all the would-be writers who think talent has something to do with financial hardship and substance-abuse issues.

POKE: The establishment in the food court that makes you momentarily wonder why anyone would want to get jabbed and prodded, before you take a moment to remember that raw-fish salad suddenly became a thing.

POKÉMON: Massive video-game and merchandising franchise built around cartoon monsters that are captured and trained to battle each other. You may want to ask yourself why your children so thoroughly relate to this basic premise.

POKÉMON GO: See previous entry; add injuries and the occasional Darwin Award death.

POKER:

WHEN PLAYING THIS GAME OF CHANCE NOT ONLINE, BUT IN A BACK ROOM OR CASINO, IT BECOMES A REFRESHINGLY ANALOG WAY FOR IDIOTS TO LOSE THEIR SHIRTS.

POLITICALLY CORRECT: A phrase used by racist, sexist, and homophobic idiots to complain that, because the phrase exists, they don't get to be racist, sexist, or homophobic anymore.

POLITICS: Activities associated with administering governance or attaining power. Such as, you know, trying to find marriage material, sucking up to the boss, or seeing how much you can get away with as a teenager. Oh, and then there's running for office, but whatever.

POMEGRANATE:

A MAGIC HEALTH-GIVING ELIXIR
SENT BY GOD TO AFFIRM THAT
YOU WERE MEANT TO PAY
ELEVEN TIMES MORE THAN
THE GOING RATE FOR
JUICE.

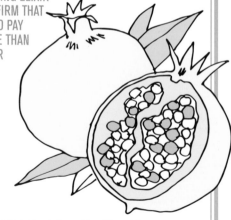

POPCORN:
WHAT PASSES FOR ROUGHAGE
IN THE DIET OF AN IDIOT.

POPULISM:
Demonstrating
solidarity with the
concerns of ordinary
people. Most often
espoused by
privileged career
politicians whose
country clubs keep
the ordinary
people out.

POP-UP STORE:
Something that is heavily promoted on social media and
then disappears. Sounds like everybody, really.

PORN: A form of motion-picture entertainment whose
paper-thin plot lines are now officially more complex
than anything you can find at your neighborhood
multiplex.

POSSESSIONS: One's belongings, one's property. One's millstones. One's useless accoutrements. One's base projections of one's insecurities about death. Other than that, they're pretty cool.

POST OFFICE: The only place where the lines are longer than they are at a theme park, but at least when you're done you've sent a package to a loved one instead of waiting two hours to spend 90 seconds on a lame-ass ride.

POSTER: The item that passes for artwork on your walls until you reach such an age as to no longer have roommates.

POSTMORTEM: Though literally referring to the examination of a body after death, this term has also come to mean any stepping back and reassessment of a business or life situation that has gone wrong. Because trying to figure out how your marriage failed so epically is best achieved by picturing it lying stiff and swollen on a slab.

POTENTIAL: Go ahead, you can tap that.

POTTER, HARRY: Boy wizard whose achievements include fighting evil, flying on a broom, and singlehandedly staving off the death of reading for at least a couple of generations.

POTUS: President of the United States. Too bad acronyms weren't big in George Washington's time, because he would have rocked this one.

POWER: As the 19th century's Lord Acton of England warned, absolute power corrupts absolutely. Unfortunately, the people most susceptible to this condition have a good laugh about it being a warning, since most of them choose to see it as a kick-ass inspirational motto.

PREGNANCY ULTRASOUND: The very embodiment of mankind's insatiable need to eradicate mystery.

PRIDE: The thing that always goes before a fall. Unless you are at a pride parade, where it always comes after the backless chaps.

PRIVACY: Something even idiots know we don't have anymore.

PROACTIVE: Because just being active is, apparently, not freaking enough.

PRODUCTION COMPANY LOGOS: The cute, hip little graphics that can number anywhere from six to sixteen and take up the first five minutes of any movie-viewing experience.

PROFESSIONAL ATHLETES: People who have hoodwinked all of us into believing that God has taken time out from dealing with world hunger and the weather to personally intervene in every clutch play they ever make.

PROFILE PICTURE: Something you have, at this writing, changed more times than your underwear. And I mean since childhood.

PROLLY: Diminutive of "probably." Part of the 21st century's goal to make every word we say sound like it is being uttered from a dentist's chair.

PROMISE: Noun: A declaration of intent that one assures one will carry out. Verb: An indicator of something good that is likely to occur. Let's use both in a sentence! "The star high school athlete promised that he would show great promise but soon learned that his best years were behind him and went into real estate."

PROPAGANDA: Everything, let's face it.

PROSTATE: The gland that starts to give out on men right around the time women stop getting bothered with the lifelong pain of their periods. Ah, sweet revenge.

PROSTITUTE: One who exchanges sex for money. And not to claim that corporate marketing is affecting the profession, but apparently you can now save money by bundling.

PSYCHIC: One who claims to be able to intuit your inner self and therefore predict your future. Probably just exceedingly good at knowing that we all want more money and more love and have someone in our lives at any given moment who is a total pain in the butt.

PSYCHO: Title of a classic Alfred Hitchcock suspense film that became a catch-all term for anyone who might be prone to dress up as their mother and murder strangers in a shower. Or, you know, compulsively Google their ex.

PUB: Like a bar, but with idiots who are a little more colorful.

PUBLIC RELATIONS: A job that tasks its practitioners with making sure a business or public figure maintains a favorable image in the media. Always an oil spill or ill-advised experiment with bestiality away from the most challenging work of their career.

PUBLISHER'S CLEARING HOUSE®: A kind of lottery that somehow always bypasses you and gets awarded to a gap-toothed inbred in a trailer park.

PUMPKIN SPICE: A flavor enhancement appearing so prevalently from October to Christmas that you probably saw it advertised on that tampon package.

PUNDITS: The only people who matter less than the ultimately disposable situations they are weighing in on.

PURPOSE: Something we are all urged to discover by people whose sole purpose is to go around saying that we're all supposed to discover our purpose.

QUIET: Still, hushed, making little to no noise. A condition human beings are so afraid of that they will take drastic measures to fill it, up to and including listening to prog rock.

QUIET DESPERATION: A state of silent, unfulfilled longing in which most of us reside, as identified by Henry David Thoreau. He clearly did not know how lucky he was, since dealing with a lot of noisy desperate people would be a huge pain in the ass.

QUIZ: A test given to students to assess their knowledge of a given subject. Often combined with the prefix "pop," to indicate a surprise test that no one was told they had to study for and therefore will probably fail like the idiots they are.

QUOTIDIAN: The ordinary, mundane, or everyday. Yes, I know, but just accept it, life will be easier that way.

RACE: An issue that will be finally and fully resolved when we learn that the Caucasian population in the United States is well on its way to becoming a minority. Oh, wait. . . .

RAIN:

MOISTURE IN THE ATMOSPHERE THAT APPEARS VISIBLY AS STREAKS OF LIQUID. IT WILL SOON CONSUME US ALL IN A CLIMATE-CHANGE-INDUCED APOCALYPTIC FLOOD, AT WHICH POINT WE SHOULD PROBABLY SET A RAIN DATE FOR OUR YARD SALES.

RAISIN: Perhaps the single most important food in the world. Because, as we know, everything happens for a raisin.

RATIONAL: Well-reasoned, sound, reasonable, prudent, drawing upon a variety of considered factors. Happened once in the early 19th century.

RAVE: Young people. Drugs. Thumping techno music. Two and a half square feet. What could go wrong?

REALITY: Things as they actually are. And we idiots usually make of that what we will.

REALITY TV: A medium that has about as much relation to reality as The Olive Garden® does to Italian food.

REBEL: An iconoclast who patently refuses to honor the accepted conventions of society. This stance has resulted in great world revolutions or—in the case of most of the idiots you know who claim to be rebels— tossing their soft-drink cups out the car window and refusing to help with the rent.

RECLINE: The position on the airline seat used by thoughtless idiots who have no qualms about pushing your tray table further into your damn lap.

RECUSE: To remove a judge or legal official from a case owing to conflict of interest. With a system as corrupt as ours, why a good recusing doesn't happen every nine seconds remains a mystery.

RECYCLING: The service that makes the alcoholic neighbor who wakes you up every morning as he tosses out his empties simply another part of saving the planet.

RELATIVES: The weddings-and-funerals crowd.

RELIEF: That flood of reassurance you feel after no longer being consumed by stress, such as when your blood tests come back clear, or when that band your friend is in didn't suck.

RELIGION: A system of faith or worship, often revolving around a central supernatural being. Which begs the question, why the hell aren't there more churches built to honor werewolves?

RENT: A monthly expense that idiot homeowners forget means somebody else has to fix all the stuff that breaks.

REPORTERS: Vital components in a democracy that make the citizenry aware of issues that could affect their lives. No wonder the White House has no use for them.

RESENTMENT: Holding on to old grudges in lieu of voicing complaint. Happily, if you do this long enough, it will manifest in any number of physical ailments, at which point you will really have something to complain about.

RESPONSIBILITY: A demonstration of one's willingness to be accountable for one's actions. A quality severely lacking in children, adolescents, young adults, adults, middle-aged people, and the elderly.

RETIREMENT: Leaving the world of the employed for good. A drastic decision that ultimately leads to the tragic outcome of wearing clashing colors, cramming onto bus tours of Tuscany, and considering joint replacement because you're covered for it now.

RETIREMENT PLAN: The prudent setting aside of funds that steadily amass into a hefty sum, which should get you through the first two weeks of being out of the workforce.

RHETORIC: Language designed to be persuasive, but often empty and insincere. Given that this is the accepted mode of speech for both first dates and political campaigns, is it any wonder our relationships are as screwed up as our public policy?

RICH: Those who can afford to buy organic produce.

RIGHT ON: Once an emphatic expression of solidarity with a righteous cause. Now, blasé commentary on such minor achievements as buying a new bong or deciding to actually pay for music.

RING:

A BAND OF METAL WORN AROUND THE THIRD FINGER OF ONE'S LEFT HAND TO INDICATE THE PROMISE OF BETROTHAL. ALONG WITH THE PROMISE OF SOME HALF-DECENT RESALE VALUE SHOULD THINGS GO UTTERLY SOUTH.

RING, THE: Groundbreaking 2002 horror film about a videotape that kills people. The only thing scary about it now is that it involves VHS.

RISK: A gamble; a situation that exposes one to potential danger or failure. It is only through great risk that we can obtain the great rewards. No, no, you go ahead. I'm interested to see how you make out.

ROBOT: Humanoid contraptions that are already being placed in real jobs and will soon be poised to take over the world. At least if our politicians are any indication.

ROCK 'N' ROLL:

THE STUFF THAT WAS USED TO PISS OFF YOUR PARENTS
BEFORE RAP AND HIP-HOP CAME ALONG.

ROOMBA®: Round robotic vacuum cleaner that you apparently bought before you realized your apartment has a crapload of right angles.

ROTARY PHONE: A now antiquated piece of technology that nonetheless made it impossible for your next-door neighbor to pace around in his back yard talking in full voice on a cell phone at five o'clock in the morning.

ROTTEN TOMATOES®: Film review site that has the power to make or break a movie's opening weekend by compiling an aggregate of opinions from a bunch of barely sentient bloggers who only leave the house to see movies they can't wait to hate.

RUDE: Discourteous; ill-mannered. Such behavior is usually only confined to parking lots, movie theater lines, highways, supermarkets, restaurants, airports, train stations, bathrooms, acts of Congress, one's own home, and any other location or circumstance you would care to mention around the entire globe and probably in outer space by now, too.

RULES: The accepted regulations that govern conduct within any given segment of society. Routinely broken by megalomaniacal politicians and the people who tie you up while they rob your house. Not that the two are related.

RUNNING MATE: Highly paid afterthought.

SAD: Despondent, crestfallen, gloomy, dejected, downcast, forlorn, melancholy, miserable, despairing Jesus no wonder you don't have any friends.

SAFETY DEMONSTRATION: The portion of air travel in which we all pay no attention to the poor flight attendants, who must feel like ignored actors in a play that closes on opening night.

SAID NO ONE EVER: Glib, kicky way to indicate that a hypothetical quotation reflects something so undesirable that no one would ever utter the quotation in the first place. Like so many other things in life, once it was discovered by the advertising industry, it became very, very annoying.

SALAD: A supposedly healthful alternative to more-fatty foods that is consistently rendered laughable when preceded by the mayonnaise-centric words "potato," "egg," and "macaroni."

SALAD BAR: Six parts lettuce, thirty-nine parts all-you-can-eat crapola.

SALESPEOPLE: A vaguely necessary component of a market-driven economy that nonetheless requires all its practitioners to attain an advanced certification in Annoying Idiot.

SALT: According to the Bible, salt is the substance that Lot's wife was turned into for her great sin of putting everyone at risk for heart attack and stroke due to excessive intake of sodium. I think.

SANCTUARY CITY: A repository for the eight or nine open-minded people still left within any given 50-mile radius.

SANTA CLAUS: A jolly, fat distributor of toys and gifts designed to introduce your idiot children to levels of materialism and greed they might not otherwise develop without him.

SATELLITE: An entity that hovers above, constantly collecting data that may one day be used against us. But we're fine with this because it is exactly the same relationship we had with our parents.

SATELLITE TV: Entertainment for people unconcerned about what space-bound alien life form may be getting privy to their rather disgusting viewing habits.

SATURDAY: The day set aside for wondering how the hell we went from sleeping until four in the afternoon after a night of debauchery to getting up at dawn in order to finish the yard work so the kids can get to the Climb 'n Slide® by ten.

SCHADENFREUDE: A term that makes us grateful that idiots do not know German.

SCHOOL: A system of organized education designed to introduce your idiot children to levels of peer pressure and mind-numbing standardized testing they might not otherwise develop without it.

SCIENCE: The systematic study of the physical and cosmic worlds based on experimentation and observation. Has given us pasteurization, the internal combustion engine, and the polio vaccine. But you're right, idiots: who needs it?

SCRAPBOOKING:

THOUGH ABOUT AS FAR FROM ACTING OUT AS YOU CAN GET, ONE GETS THE SENSE THAT PEOPLE WHO ENGAGE IN THIS MIND-NUMBING HOBBY CONSIDER IT THEIR VERSION OF DRINKING HARD AND PARTYING HARDER.

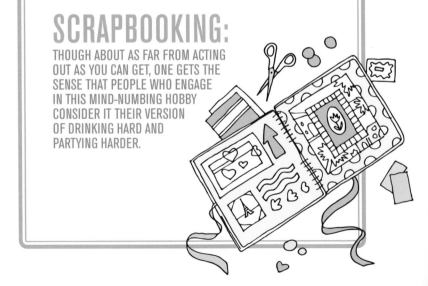

SCREEN SAVER: The image on the home screen of your computer. Usually the place where you upload a photograph of your spouse and children in order to convince everyone that they are more important to you than the montage of DC Universe characters you really wanted on that stupid screen.

SCREENPLAY: Something that is, at any given moment, being worked on by your dentist, lawyer, gardener, or barista.

SECOND: The single unit of time we employ to measure how long it takes to scream at our computers for being so slow.

SECOND CHANCE: What everyone deserves. Except that one idiot.

SECRETARY: One who assists with correspondence, record-keeping, appointment-setting, and supplying spouses with fictional whereabouts for their employer, who is currently boffing someone at the Radisson during lunch.

SELF-CENTERED: Well, the alternative would be "Other People-Centered," and that ain't happening anytime soon.

SELF-CHECKOUT: A way to avoid the time-consuming hassle of completing your transaction with a cashier, while taking six times as long to complete your transaction with fickle, glitch-laden computers and the single, harried ex-cashier assigned to deal with all of them.

SELF-DOUBT: The constant negating force that makes us question every decision and holds us back from moving forward in our lives. God, I can't believe I just said something so stupid!

SELF-DRIVING CARS: Innovative technology that will radically reduce the amount of people who might die in traffic accidents. Hardly worth radically reducing the fun we get from hoping the idiot who just cut us off will die in a traffic accident.

SELF-ESTEEM: The need for a sense of one's own worth that the Greatest Generation would have laughed at anybody actually admitting to, but then that's probably why they were the Greatest Generation.

SELF-HELP: A way to solve one's personal or emotional problems by purchasing books with such titles as *I Lied About How Easy it is to Overcome My Problems, and So Can You.*

SELFHOOD: Really? We need a word to let us know we're a self? Well, perhaps it is safer than hurling yourself into a brick wall just to make sure you're here.

SELFIE: A photo of oneself taken on a camera phone. Often used to commemorate being present at some hugely significant location, such as the Grand Canyon or the Sunglass Hut at the mall.

SELFIE STICK:

THE TOOL USED TO EXTEND YOUR CAMERA PHONE A LITTLE FURTHER, THUS PROVIDING A HANDY TOOL THAT ALLOWS YOU AND A BUNCH OF OTHER TOOLS TO BE IN THE SAME TOOL-LADEN PHOTO.

SEPTEMBER: The month that ushers in fall, yes, but mostly the title of an Earth, Wind & Fire song that elicits a chemical response allowing humans to feel happy for three tiny minutes of their sorry, screwed-up lives.

SERENITY: A state of tranquility and calmness involving a still and empty mind. Ironically, this is the one thing most easily achieved by idiots.

SEX: The universe's way of making sure we look our most idiotic while doing the thing that gives us the most pleasure.

SEX SCENE: Obligatory two minutes of arched backs and heads dropping down below-frame that occurs in most R-rated movies and gives everyone in the theater the same awkward feeling of wishing they had waited for the DVD.

SEXT: A text message with overtly sexual content. Or, as it is known in divorce court: evidence, you idiot.

SHAKESPEARE, WILLIAM: Born in the 16th century, Shakespeare is still considered to be the world's greatest writer, as evidenced by the fact that millions of students each year Google the plot synopses of his plays rather than having to deal with reading them.

SHAMAN: In tribal cultures, a powerful and gifted person who can traverse among the realm of the spirits. In pop culture, basically anybody who paid one of those websites to name a constellation after them.

SHAME: A feeling of inner humiliation caused by the awareness of having done something wrong. Since our society contains no more awareness of having done something wrong, we're good.

SHARING: Opening up. Letting others know how you feel. Conveying a sense of your true self. Emptying the room.

SHARK: Majestic sea predator that was doing fine before someone decided to add *nado* to the end of its name.

SHART: Adorable hybrid word implying that a fart has crossed over into something more substantial. Because we apparently just went too long without being able to adequately describe this charming phenomenon.

SHAWSHANK REDEMPTION, THE: Consistently highly ranked motion picture based on a Stephen King story and containing the thought-provoking line "Get busy living, or get busy dying." Hey, if the dude who came up with a horrific clown that lives in a storm drain, a psychotic woman who kidnaps and tortures a writer, and a crazy axe murderer who is possessed by a haunted hotel can summon an uplifting thought like that, what's your freaking problem?

SHOEHORN: To force an object or idea to fit into a space that will not accommodate it. Perhaps the only verb in existence to be named after an implement that no one has used since the Johnson administration.

SHOES: Footwear. And if you have the ongoing compulsion to own more than two pairs of them per week, you might want to walk your designer feet into a 12-Step program.

SHOPPING: A hideous, mind-numbing activity that enough idiots find pleasant to help prop up our crumbling infrastructure.

SHOPPING CART: A conveyance for various items. Supermarkets now program it to kill any homeless person who attempts to drag it out of the parking lot.

SHORT ATTENTION SPAN: The inability to focus on any one thing for more than a few moments. Actually comes in pretty handy when you think about how depressed you can get from focusing on any one thing for more than a few moments.

SHORTS: Okay, men, they're like down to our ankles now, so, like, when will someone finally admit that we should stop calling them "short"?

SHOWER: What we persist in telling people we are going to "jump" into, even no one has ever done more than step into one.

SHREDDING: Something you can do to paper or cabbage, or while playing a guitar. The first might foil a government investigation; the second will yield cole slaw, and the third requires hair. Lots and lots of hair.

SIDE EYE: Apparently, a shortened version of "side of the eye" was needed because by the 22nd century, everything will be required to be described in two words or less.

SILVER: A designation added to various products aimed at the elderly and handily replacing golden in much the same way that oldies became classic rock.

SILVER LINING: What every cloud is said to have, as a way of encouraging you to hold out until the next crushing defeat that never does reveal its upside, either.

SIN: Let he who is without this amoral condition cast the first stone. And cast it really, really hard, dude, because we totally deserve it.

SIRI: The talking, information-finding app on one's iPhone that has yet to sufficiently answer the question "Siri, can you find me a human being to interact with?" *See also:* Alexa.

SISTER: Either a female sibling or a nun. And if you are dating the former, you better treat her like the latter, you punk.

SKATEBOARDING: Injury-laden recreational activity that got bumped to the level of a competitive sport so that stoners could feel like football players for a few minutes.

SKILL SET: Phrase invented by employers who need to politely tell interviewees that they possess no skills whatsoever.

SKYDIVING: One of the featured chapters in the well-known informational book series, *Attempted Suicide for Dummies.*

SLEEPING: Something that amoral a-holes never have any trouble doing, whereas you lie awake fretting over a candy bar you stole when you were four.

SMARTPHONE:
YOU ARE ITS BITCH, IN CASE YOU DIDN'T KNOW.

SMH: Acronym for *Shaking My Head*. A way to convey righteous indignation at some foolish thing on the Internet by using some foolish acronym on the Internet.

SMILE: A facial expression of gladness. Smiling at everyone you pass each day is a wonderful way to make them think you were dropped on your head as a child.

SMOKING: 1. The act of drawing tobacco fumes into one's lungs. 2. Common prefix to the word "hot," to indicate an especially attractive person. 3. Both lie in wait to kill you in very different ways.

SNAPCHAT: Mobile app that allows users to send photos or videos that are gone from memory after ten seconds. Excellent way to prepare the nation's youth for Alzheimer's.

SNEAKERS: As with most things in life, sneakers remained sadly unfulfilling until they could at last contain an LED light-up function.

SOAP: A cleansing agent that thoughtfully adds anti-bacterial properties to its pump dispensers so that idiots can become less resistant to bacteria.

SOBRIETY: The state of being sober for various lengths of time. Often ridiculed by idiots who tease you about drinking a ginger ale just so they can overcompensate for their own sorry, untreated-alcoholic lives.

SOCIAL MEDIA: Given that "media" is the collective term for the news outlets that befuddle us on a daily basis, and that "social" implies actually interacting with another human being, this term is built on a bigger foundation of lies than most marriages.

SOFT DRINKS: Carbonated, non-alcoholic beverages that often not only contain more addictive substances than their liquored-up counterparts but also are available in single-serving half-gallon cups for those who want to hasten their demise with something other than alcohol.

SOFTWARE: The most intricate, intellectually complicated item that has ever been so glaringly and obviously designed by idiots.

SONG: Merely words set to music. Unless you are an adolescent, in which case it not only defines your very being, but also, upon the discovery that your classmate likes something else, provides a perfectly valid reason for ending a perfectly good friendship.

SOUL: 1. The spiritual essence of a living thing. 2. A style of R&B-influenced music. 3. If you don't like 2, you ain't got a 1.

SOUL PATCH: A tiny tuft of hair underneath a man's lower lip. Sort of like an eye patch, except what it's covering is what the man looked like before he decided to resemble his own pubes.

SOUND BITE: What we are all just waiting to become, depending on who has their camera phone handy when we lose it at the mall food court.

SPELL-CHECK: The function on your computer that you keep forgetting can't figure out context, you idiot.

SPELLING: Something idiots don't care about anymore.

SPIRITUAL: What people who are not religious usually claim to be. And they may be right, because at our essences we are not physical beings having a spiritual experience, but spiritual beings who cannot believe all the amazing crap we get to buy.

SPOILER ALERT: Giving notice on key information in a story that might take away the surprise of experiencing it for the first time. Here's a spoiler alert for you: we die in the end.

SPORTS: The only part of a newscast that actually reports facts.

SPOTIFY: Yet another outlet providing musicians the opportunity to lose money. Hey, at least now you have some insight into why they always need to crash on your couch.

SPRING: A time of great promise. Which really could be any time you'd care to designate; however, the sting of grinding that promise into the dirt with your own stupidity seems to be greater in spring.

STALKER: An idiot who nonetheless has the stamina to sit in a parked car for a very, very long time.

STANDARDS: A set of markers for excellence. One should always hold oneself to a higher standard than one expects of anyone else. In so doing, one is virtually guaranteeing oneself a long, rich life of passive-aggressive, self-flagellating martyrdom.

STAND-UP SPECIAL: Thanks to Netflix, something your dog could potentially have.

STAR TREK: Science fiction juggernaut whose entire fan base has never boldly gone anywhere, let alone where no man has gone before.

STAR WARS: Science fiction juggernaut whose entire fan base forgave George Lucas for the roughly nine hours of crap he released during the late 1990s and early 2000s.

STARBUCKS®: The coffee place where the jacked-up prices are justified by the extra effort the employees go to in calling out your name.

STATE-OF-THE-ART: Already obsolete.

STATS: A string of facts and numerical data that sports fans discuss ad nauseam, clinging to the belief that they actually amount to anything. Not that different from what we'll all do when our lives flash before our eyes, so thanks for the heads up, guys.

STATUE: Stone sculpture commonly placed in a park or public square, and featuring the full-body likeness of some old-money historical figure who probably would never have allowed the likes of you to live in his town.

STATUS UPDATE: A report on your latest activities as posted to social media. It is hardly a coincidence that the word "status" appears in this term, since the feeble amount of Likes you got clearly reveals that you have none.

STOCK MARKET: The place where your money becomes imaginary, and then eventually becomes real again when you lose it all.

STOIC: The practice of enduring pain and hardship without conveying any outward feelings. Usually means that by the time your loved ones realize you're having a heart attack, it will be too late.

STOP SIGN: The red, hexagonal road marking that is blown through more times than . . . well, let's stop there. This is a family book.

STORY: What each of us is encouraged to understand that we have; that the events of our life are interesting and powerful enough to fuel a compelling narrative as thrilling and passionate as a novel like *War and Peace*. Well, more like *Everyone Poops*, but whatever you need to believe.

ST. PATRICK'S DAY: A 24-hour period during which, they say, everyone is a little bit Irish. Which apparently confers upon each of us the right to throw up in the street, regardless of our ethnic heritage.

STRANGER: Nothing more than a friend you haven't yet met. And if you still believe this tragically naïve little sentiment in the 21st century, you have earned a place in the Dictionary of Idiocy.

STRATEGIZE: To get together with one or more persons and discuss options for punching in the face the next person who uses the word "strategize."

STREAMING MEDIA: A technology that introduced the world to the term "buffering."

STRESS: Emotional strain caused by trying circumstances. In every stressful situation, simply ask yourself the question "Will this matter after I am dead?" Then, when the answer is "yes," continue with the stressful situation.

STUDY: Either the act of devoting time to gaining knowledge, or the room in which you do it. Both make you fall asleep and wake up realizing you will fail the test, so the distinction is fairly moot.

STUPID: Lacking innate intelligence or common sense. Or, as the word is known to our public officials, voters.

STUPID QUESTIONS: Something that management professes there are none of in their employee-feedback sessions, thereby causing everyone who is about to ask a stupid question to clam up.

SUBCONSCIOUS: The part of the brain that is not entirely aware of what is motivating it. But it's usually your wounded inner idiot, so start from there the next time you try to stab someone with a fork for simply asking whether or not you got a haircut.

SUBTITLES: A movie's way of keeping idiots out of the theater.

SUCCESS: Something that only comes to us after many disappointments. At which time we are too bitter and pissed off to appreciate it.

SUCK IT UP, BUTTERCUP: Phrase originating among World War II pilots, who were urged to suck up any vomit expelled into their oxygen masks lest they risk death by inhaling the resulting acidic fumes. Sure makes smug politicians and your unfeeling friends seem even more like privileged, ignorant idiots, doesn't it?

SUCKS: In yet another example of the removal of context from public discourse, here we have an obscenity that has become a perfectly acceptable expression of displeasure at an object or situation, so common that it is even used by children—who no doubt remain uninformed about the creating-a-partial-vacuum-with-your-mouth imagery that inspired it.

SUNDAY: The day on which God rested and the day on which we honor God by contributing heavily to our retail-based economy.

SUFFERING: Pain and agony caused by physical or emotional hardship. Why God allows this has been debated by many a theologian, but it is still easier to explain than how to get a job on LinkedIn.

SUGAR: Sweetener added to almost everything, in quantities you should be very diligent about checking labels for—since the items with lower amounts of sugar are probably going to taste like crap.

SUMMER: Three months of squeezing in a bunch of "activities" in order to enjoy some "quality time" with your "loved ones."

SUN: Daily overseer of the melanoma lottery.

SUNSCREEN: Products that put the highest number possible on their packaging in order to screen out 75 percent of idiocy's harmful rays.

SUPER BOWL: Annual football competition that reminds its fans they don't know how to read Roman numerals.

SUPERFOOD: Nutrient-rich food touted for its benefits to our health, added in minuscule amounts to just about anything in order to make us think that simply by ingesting it we will induce a grade-A colon blow.

SUPERMARKET: The place where a small portion of any given aisle could feed three hundred disadvantaged children for a week. But, hey, it's worth it to exercise our freedom of choice on which of the eighty-seven types of granola bars we would rather purchase.

SUPREME COURT:

NINE PEOPLE FROM MANY DIFFERENT WALKS OF LIFE EXCEPT
REALLY ESSENTIALLY THE SAME WALK OF LIFE WHO GET
TO DECIDE WHAT PEOPLE WHO ARE ACTUALLY FROM MANY
DIFFERENT WALKS OF LIFE WILL NOT BE ALLOWED TO DO.

SURVEILLANCE: The government's way of letting you know that your dead family members are not the only ones looking down on you as you play with yourself.

SUSHI: Might need to fact-check this, but pretty sure "sushi" is Japanese for "food-borne pathogens."

SVU: Also, *Law & Order: SVU* or *Special Victims Unit.* Long-running police procedural in the *Law & Order* franchise that allows you to identify which of your friends are way creepier than you thought they were.

SWEET!: Exclamation meant to convey a favorable response to whatever information has just been relayed. Has now lost all meaning, since it is often blurted out in response to everything from cancer going into remission to being granted extra foam on your latte.

SWIMMING POOL: The only impractical accoutrement that is more high-maintenance than a supermodel girlfriend.

SWIPE LEFT: To zip past someone's photo on a dating site, thereby declaring them utterly undesirable. Not that social networking duplicates the cripplingly cruel dynamic of junior high school or anything.

T-SHIRT: An item usually emblazoned with a logo, a band name, or a movie or TV character. So, basically, you paid money to a copyrighted entity in order that they could enjoy free advertising at your expense. Nice one.

TABLET: A computer device that not only looks nothing like the pad of paper it is meant to mimic, but also shares a name with drugs distributed in pill form. You do the math.

TAI CHI: The Chinese exercise regimen of slow, deliberate movements that makes everyone else in the park think you are out of your tiny little mind.

TAILGATING: Following too closely behind the vehicle in front of you. Sadly, the practice shows no signs of diminishing, even in the face of such imposing deterrents as those Yosemite Sam "Back Off" mud flaps.

TAKEOUT: The option chosen when the prospect of having nothing to say to each other across the kitchen table is a little less heinous than the prospect of having nothing to say to each other across the restaurant table.

TALKING: Something idiots do way too much of and non-idiots do way too little to nip in the bud.

TALKING POINT: Invitation to a brawl.

TARGET®: Somewhere between Bergdorf Goodman® and Walmart®.

TAXES: The money we give the government to help pay for the services they refuse to give us.

TEA: The all-powerful elixir of Great Britain, offered as a soothing balm for everything from a bad hair day to being diagnosed with a terminal illness.

TEA, HERBAL: The stuff that is kept under the counter at coffee shops for when the weirdos show up.

TEACHABLE MOMENT: A key juncture at which an opportunity for growth and learning presents itself. A term used by the media to point out the tragic irony of the idiots who quite willfully choose not to avail themselves of this opportunity every five minutes or so.

TEACHER:

AN INDISPENSABLE COMPONENT OF SOCIETY, AS EVIDENCED BY THE FACT THAT WE CAN ALL REMEMBER AT LEAST ONE TEACHER WHO CHANGED OUR LIVES BY SUBCONSCIOUSLY CONVEYING THAT WE SHOULD NEVER BE A TEACHER IF WE WANT TO GET RICH.

TECHNOLOGY: Blanket term for all those things that make us want to smash all those things with a ball-peen hammer.

TED TALKS: Sort of the "You Might Be a Redneck If . . ." routine, but for hipsters.

TEAM BUILDING: A management-sponsored gathering of co-workers, designed to create incentives for greater workplace productivity. And about as forced and insincere as an "I'll-call-you" after a one-night stand.

TEAM PLAYER: Suck up.

TELEMARKETER: Someone you really kind of have to admire for the sheer balls they must have to not only bug the crap out of you, but also bug the crap out of many hundreds like you every day.

TESLA: Company that manufactures premium electric cars, solar panels, and other innovative technology, named after the pioneering scientist Nikola Tesla in honor of the fact that he died penniless and thus cannot access, or, more importantly, go to court over, the millions being made in his memory.

TEXTING: Probably the most unforeseen use of opposable thumbs since the prologue to Kubrick's *2001: A Space Odyssey.*

THANK YOU: A phrase that is uttered countless times each day by retail clerks, and yet your ungrateful children will probably never voice it until that one poignant moment at your bedside in the assisted living facility.

THANK-YOU CARD: An admirable old school greeting from someone who appreciates your kindness in not telling them that their charming dial-up greeting will end up in recycling post haste.

THANK YOU FOR YOUR SERVICE: The "Have a Nice Day" of civilian interactions with members of the military.

THANKSGIVING: Proof that the only way idiots could think of dealing with other idiots was to suggest that they all gather for a meal.

THEY'RE/THEIR/THERE: Three versions of something that sounds the same, but is, actually, three different words. Idiots, take note.

THEME PARK: A place to drop a month's pay on something you could easily do at home, for example, waiting hours for something interesting to happen while ingesting crappy food and getting increasingly irritated with your so-called loved ones.

THINKING: What we idiots spend way too much time doing about ultimately unimportant things and virtually no time doing about matters of great consequence. Try not to think about it.

THOUGHT: See previous entry, add some incomprehensible process involving neurons or something, as if that makes it okay.

THRIFT STORE: Once a go-to establishment in which those who have fallen on hard times could buy the clothing and appliances they need to keep their family at survival level. Now an antique mart run by people whose idea of thrift is to make sure that the only people who will ever come through the door are hipsters who will pay through the nose for a mid-century modern end table.

THROWBACK THURSDAY: A social networking tradition that helps your friends understand how you were even more of a douchebag fifteen years ago than you are today.

THROWING SHADE: Talking trash about another person. Part and parcel to this slang phrase is that it reflects more poorly on the shade thrower than it does on the shade receiver. However, if by now you have ceased to care about either of these two idiots, then by all means throw shade at both of them.

THURSDAY: Because it makes us breathlessly anticipate the end of the workweek, Thursday achieves its best qualities simply because of its proximity to something exciting. Sort of like the drummer in a rock 'n' roll band.

TICKETS: Either penalties imposed upon you by the enforcement of motor vehicle codes, or proofs-of-purchase that allow you admission to various events. Hard to say which one is the bigger rip-off.

TINDER™: Mobile app used for casual sex hookups. And never more than a heartbeat away from the ever-popular boiled bunny rabbit scenario.

TIPPING POINT: The juncture at which a series of small events leads to a larger, more significant one. Whether you are about to reach this point with donuts is entirely up to you.

TODAY: The first day of the rest of your life. Which simply must mean that it's the final day of the last ten years of unrelenting suckfest, right? Right? Anybody?

TODDLER: A parent's assurance that they will not go to hell when they die, as even Satan fully respects that they have been through hell already.

TOILET: The conveyance that whisks your bodily waste away to an undisclosed location, thereby allowing you to give less than two sh*ts about where it ends up.

TOILET, PUBLIC: The place where prominently posted signs allow idiots to believe that the employees are actually washing their hands before returning to work.

TOLKIEN, J.R.R.: Author of *The Hobbit* and *The Lord of the Rings* trilogy. Indirectly responsible for the most reckless overuse of CGI in the 21st century to date.

TOOTHBRUSH: The first throw-down in the "Let's Try this Cohabitating Thing" sweepstakes.

TOP-TEN LIST: A collection of the ten most important or significant things associated with any given topic. If this form of information-gathering were to be suddenly removed from the Internet, the world would be left with roughly four websites.

TOTES: Diminutive of "totally," used to express enthusiastic agreement and to let others know you are a douchebag.

TOWN HALL: A chance for the general public to further cement their distrust of elected officials.

TOXIC: Co-workers, relationships, chemicals. If only the government paid out trillions in damages for the first two.

TOYS: TINY ITEMS WE THROW A TANTRUM TO RECEIVE AS CHILDREN; VERY LARGE ITEMS WE THROW OUR SAVINGS AWAY TO RECEIVE AS ADULTS.

TRAFFIC: Something about which nothing can be done, yet something we waste precious minutes, even hours, wishing were not occurring. Good preparation for death, when you think about it.

TRAGEDY: What people who *feel* see life as, in contrast to those who *think*, who see life as a comedy. At least according to the 18th-century Englishman Horace Walpole, who is now dead, which is kind of ironically funny. I think.

TRAILER: The coming attraction for a movie, in which all the best parts of the film are condensed into two and a half minutes, in order to distract us from the fact that there are only two and a half good minutes in the whole stupid film.

TRAIN:

QUAINT FORM OF TRANSPORTATION ADORED BY PEOPLE WHO LIKE TO PICTURE THE SIMPLER TIMES WHEN A VANISHED BREED OF GREAT MEN HAD A VISION TO CONNECT OUR NATION USING MILLIONS OF EXPLOITED IMMIGRANTS.

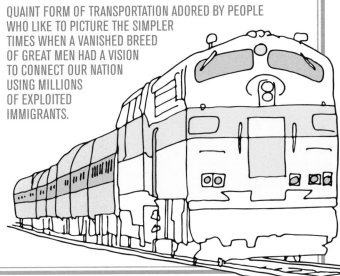

TRAIN WRECK: Catch-all term used to indicate a person or situation that has gone terribly wrong. If you have never encountered such a scenario in life, then congratulations: you have not yet worked with, slept with, or paid money to see a movie made by an idiot.

TRANS FATS: No idea. Never understood this one. Not at all moved to Google it, either.

TRANSGENDER: A man or woman who feels that the way he or she was forced to be as a child does not match up to the way he or she feels as an adult. Hmm. Relatable, much, haters?

TRASH: You can toss out the trash, you can call someone trash, you can even feel pretty trashed. Interestingly, each of these options is very well conveyed by the image of a half-eaten frozen dinner dripping rancid Bolognese sauce into a bin liner.

TREE:

SOMETHING EVEN HARDLINE CAPITALISTS MAY WANT
TO START HUGGING. JUST SO THEY CAN SAY A PROPER
GOOD-BYE.

TRENDING: About to be over.

TRIATHLON: Porn for the physical fitness crowd.

TRIVIA: Inconsequential information beloved by idiots who cannot name a single amendment in the Bill of Rights, but can instantly call up the name of Darth Maul's personal gauntlet fighter ship from the animated television series *Star Wars: Rebels*. (It's *Nightbrother*, btw.)

TRUMP, DONALD:

THE FIRST AMERICAN PRESIDENT TO PROVIDE THE PERFECT TRAINING GROUND FOR PROSPECTIVE NEW PARENTS—WHO WILL NEED A GOOD STRETCH OF PRACTICAL EXPERIENCE IN COPING WITH A PETULANT CHILD.

TRUST: What we put in our public officials, our significant others, and our Internet transactions. At least the last one has a little padlock icon to reassure us that everything is (probably) going to be fine.

TRUTH: Props to Aaron Sorkin. We really can't handle it.

TRUTHER: 21st-century term for a conspiracy theorist, perhaps meant to imply that a truther is trying to get at the truth, as opposed to simply being irrationally convinced that JFK was murdered by John Lennon.

TUESDAY: Not yet Wednesday, no longer Monday. Hardly qualifies as a day, really, but useful for the comforting realization that you still have three days to put everything off until Friday.

TURN SIGNALS: We checked, and it's okay, nobody has to use them anymore, so we're good.

TWERK: To dance in a provocative manner, usually involving the shaking of the buttocks and the thrusting of the hips. If by "provocative manner" you mean "kind of gross and rather embarrassing," then, yeah.

TWILIGHT ZONE, THE: Groundbreaking 1950s and 1960s television show that was so good at predicting what idiots we would become in the future that it makes us all feel like retroactive idiots for being such idiots back then that we didn't see the idiocy coming.

TWIN PEAKS: The only TV show that is exactly like your relationship: no matter how many times you look at it, it will never make any sense.

TWITTER: The social-media giant responsible for changing the term "pound sign" to "hashtag."

TYPOS: Things that reveal one's idiocy to potential friends, employers, or life partners. Luckily, life will soon provide a remedy to this by never requiring you to write anything ever again.

UBER: A convenient way to entrust your transportation to a potential serial killer with access to Waze.

UGLY SWEATER: Adorable holiday tradition founded upon the idea of finding yet another way to make Jesus throw up when he comes back to see what is being done in his name.

UN-AMERICAN: Inquisitive.

UNAWARE: A condition of cluelessness about another's feelings that hits at exactly the moment you agree to be in a committed relationship.

UNCONDITIONAL LOVE: Something we rely on our pets to give us, since we are incapable of giving it to each other. Or our pets for that matter, who can provoke our disdain with something as simple as taking a dump on the carpet.

UNDERSTANDING: Finding yourself being sympathetic to another's feelings. Don't you hate when that happens?

UNDER-UTILIZED: Polite term for someone who never had much to utilize to begin with.

UNDERWEAR: Garment worn over one's private parts that ranges from sexless and saggy to frilly and tantalizing. Depending upon how long a couple has been together, saggy and tantalizing could also be an option.

UNEMPLOYMENT: A despairing condition brought on by lack of available work. Just the motivation an idiot needs to vote for someone whose utter lack of caring about working people can be measured in gigaparsecs.

UFO: Proof that a good percentage of people carry enough subconscious guilt to want to be punished by a force outside themselves, and that it will be a lot more palatable if the punishment is doled out by a species other than their own.

UNFRIEND: Remove a person from your Facebook friend list. This decisive action allows you to behave just like a politician, by getting rid of anyone who disagrees with you.

UNION: Quaint little concept involving fair wages and worker representation that keeps not quite dying.

UNIQUE: What each of us thinks we are until we run into the other people at the theme park, crappy movie, or brothel.

UNITED STATES: A geographical area that is about as united as the garter snake and field mouse communities.

UNIVERSE, THE: The cosmos; all existing matter in space. And, apparently, a force that reads your energies and will give back all you need to succeed. Recent studies show that the universe is particularly receptive to old money, trust funds, and having a relative in show business.

UNPOPULAR: A once-feared social stigma that has inexplicably become the back door into being popular. Go figure.

UPCYCLE: A concept containing the rash assumption that making a tablecloth out of discarded gum wrappers is an improvement on what should have probably remained discarded.

UPLASINVIL: This is not a real word; however, it is notable as being the last fake word available to use for the name of a prescription drug product that is advertised on television. Yup, it's true. The rest have all been taken.

URGENT CARE: Medical help that sets itself apart from the traditional emergency-room experience in that the care is something you wait urgently for.

VACCINE: Life-saving medicines administered to children to keep them from developing severe diseases or, well, dying. But the pretty celebrity on the shiny TV says they are bad, so, hey, bring on the infections.

VALENTINE'S DAY: A day for romance which often punctuates feelings of loneliness in single people. But remember: if you want love to come into your life, you must first let love for yourself into your own heart, after which you can welcome the love of another into the loving space you have thus created, and through the love that you have manifested you can discover that the love blossoming in yourself is now the love you can give to the love that has been offering itself to you all along. Yes, I know, it's a kick in the head, but sometimes it's just that simple.

VAPING:

SMOKING FOR PEOPLE WHO PREFER TO RECEIVE THEIR CANCER ELECTRONICALLY.

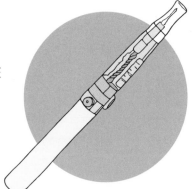

VEGAS:

VACATION DESTINATION WHERE THE PHRASE "WHAT HAPPENS IN VEGAS STAYS IN VEGAS" USED TO MEAN ILLICIT SEX AND GAMBLING, AND NOW MEANS YOU MAY WANT TO KEEP HAVING PAID $300 TO SEE A LAME-ASS VENTRILOQUIST ON THE DOWN-LOW.

VEGETABLES:

A FOOD GROUP THAT SCREAMS "HEALTH," AND IS THEREFORE AVOIDED BY IDIOTS WHO TAKE PERVERSE PRIDE IN ONLY EATING THE STUFF THAT MAY KILL THEM.

VICTORIA'S SECRET®: Yet another product line establishing an unrealistic expectation for female attractiveness. Still, if it provides enough of a release to keep your resident idiot from downloading porn, so be it.

VIDEO CONFERENCING: Cutting-edge meeting platform that offers its participants a screen mosaic of little boxes, each with its own tiny idiot.

VIDEO PIRACY: The illegal downloading of entertainment content from the Internet. An act freely engaged in by young people, who pay it even less mind than thinking about the needs of others.

VIRTUAL REALITY: Technology that allows immersion into hyper-realistic fantasy scenarios. Right. Call me when one of the hyper-realistic fantasy scenarios is having a life that is happy enough not to need this crap.

VOICEMAIL: Digital phone messaging technology employed by millions, with the exception of people in movies, who all still have answering machines so that important plot information can be relayed in voice-over.

VOTER FRAUD: An unsettling circumstance that somehow became what idiots blame when their side wins.

WALK: Unbearable exercise option that must sadly be engaged in when one has to get up to look for the remote.

WALK BACK: To retreat from one's original stance on an issue. Many a marriage, commitment to taking care of a house pet, or declared college major could have benefitted from one of these.

WALKING DEAD, THE: Both the title of a popular television show and a description of most of us, anyway. Hence the show's popularity.

WALL: Something we build around ourselves psychologically in order to keep people at a distance and avoid having to deal with the pain and self-loathing we so deeply fear. Oh, and then there's building an actual wall to keep people out, but that couldn't possibly be motivated by the same thing. Nope. No way.

WALL STREET:

EIGHT BLOCKS IN NEW YORK THAT SCREW IT ALL UP FOR THE OTHER 31 BILLION, 276 MILLION, 493 THOUSAND AND SIX BLOCKS IN THE WORLD.

WALMART®: The only retail store that is bigger than the town whose residents it serves.

WANT: What we are all big, steaming sacks of.

WAR: A hideous human trend that we keep trying to bring a stop to, but ultimately we cannot bring ourselves to deprive PBS of subjects for future *American Experience* documentaries.

WASHINGTON, GEORGE: Founding Father, first American president, and Revolutionary War general. But his greatest achievement was crossing the Potomac River while it was still unpolluted.

WASHINGTON MONUMENT: Should you require additional confirmation that the United States was settled by rich white guys, look no further than this 555-foot Caucasian penis.

WAYBACK MACHINE®: At every election cycle, what the aforementioned rich white men keep trying to cram us all into.

WAZE®: Navigation app that insists on advising its users to take a left against eight lanes of oncoming vehicles without the aid of a traffic light.

WEAKNESS: To some, shirking away from battle. To others, the inability to resist rich food. To still others, the inability to resist charming idiots. One might get you killed, the other might get you killed, and the other might get you killed, too.

WEAK SAUCE: A phrase used to describe anything of inferior quality. Or, a phrase used to describe anything.

WEALTH: Something that is better measured by what a man *is* as opposed to what a man *has*. Although if the man *has* a crapload of money, the fact that he *is* a total douche is often overlooked.

WEATHER: What Southern Californians vaguely remember.

WEBCAM: The tiny little eye built into your computer that allows the FBI to see you at best looking your slovenly worst, and at worst doing your best impersonation of a frantic, self-pleasuring monkey.

WEBINAR: A chance to sit through the same dullard in a short-sleeve shirt and tie giving an agonizing PowerPoint® that you sat through in the conference room at work, except this time there's a camera on you so you can't doze off.

WEDDING: A day on which we are often encouraged to remember the words of 1 Corinthians 13, which state that "Love is patient, love is kind, love is not envious or boastful or arrogant or rude, it does not insist on its way, it is not irritable or resentful. . . ." Basically, love is a look-at-me-I'm-so-perfect pain in the butt.

WEDDING PHOTOGRAPHER: A person gifted in the art of corralling a bunch of future enemies before they get too drunk to stand in a line.

WEDNESDAY: Colloquially referred to as "hump day," probably because by the middle of the workweek you start wondering whom you have to hump to get out of this job.

WEEK: The seven days comprising Sunday through Saturday. There are 52 of them in a year. And 1300 of them in the 25 wasted years of your life. (Adjust as needed.)

WHISPERS: Those risqué little excursions into dirty talk that your partner breathes into your ear while you try not to kill the mood by laughing.

WHITENING STRIPS: Because like every other part of our damn bodies, teeth must not be allowed to age.

WI-FI:

A SERVICE THAT TELLS THE WORLD YOU ARE WILLING TO OFFER HACKERS UNLIMITED ACCESS TO YOUR PERSONAL INFORMATION JUST SO YOU CAN ENJOY A VENTI MACCHIATO AND USE SNAPCHAT AT THE SAME TIME.

WILL: Document to be drawn up before one's death which makes the extremely rash assumption that, in this economy, you will have anything more than a futon and a coffee maker to divide among your surviving descendants.

WIN-WIN: A situation in which both parties benefit from the outcome. Commonly used by the party who knows the other party is getting screwed but wants to convince them otherwise.

WINDSHIELD WIPERS: The things that wipe your windshield. Holy crap, it took us until the W's to find something that actually *is* what it says it is.

WINE: Alcoholic beverage that allows you to use sophisticated terminology such as "full-bodied" and "bouquet" before slurring your words and passing out just like you do when you choose to drink beer instead.

WINFREY, OPRAH: Legendary daytime talk-show host who was the last person you ever allowed to put you in touch with your feelings.

WINNING: Obtaining victory in a competition. Something society places far too much value upon and which could be potentially damaging to our children, many of whom are born losers.

WINTER: The year's coldest season. During which you can always find idiots in their twenties headed out to a party in a snow squall wearing nothing but T-shirts and cocktail dresses.

WIRELESS CARRIER: A service provider whose sole purpose is to give its users something to complain about at those times when they are not sick or dying.

WISH: A desire for something that is most likely unattainable. And yes, just ten stupid minutes of peace and quiet to get some reading done on the crapper qualifies.

WITCHCRAFT: USING SPELLS AND THE INVOKING OF SPIRITS TO EFFECT OUTCOMES ON THE PHYSICAL PLANE. WHY THIS WAS NOT THE FIRST CHOICE OF WORDS TO DESCRIBE THE POLITICAL PROCESS IS SADLY UNKNOWN TO HISTORY.

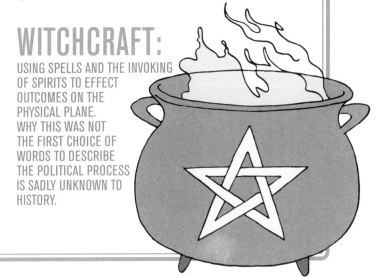

WIZARD: Either a sorcerer with magical powers or the help feature in software that automates computer functions. The first actually works.

WOKE: A word which began as a call to remain vigilant and aware about important social issues (as in "get woke"), and has already been co-opted to praise such vaguely enlightened behaviors as drinking an all-fruit smoothie or paying one's rent on time.

WOMAN: A human being routinely paid far less than her male counterparts, and who would kill for a chance to earn a nice salary for being an incompetent idiot just like they do.

WONDER: A state of wide-eyed amazement about all that is. The best way to achieve this is to experience life the way a child would. This, of course, refers to taking in everything as if for the first time, and not being largely non-verbal and crapping in your pants.

WONDER WOMAN: Superhero whose independent spirit and take-charge attitude are inspirations for strong women everywhere who should also make sure they look exceedingly damn hot in a revealing costume.

WOO-HOO!: An expression of shared enthusiasm, designed to show a friend or loved one that you are cheering them on for a great achievement in their life. Usually ends up coming out half-hearted and anemic, mostly because it requires a level of sincerity that envy and jealousy make it impossible to access.

WORDS WITH FRIENDS™: Online spelling game that allows you to show off your prodigious ability to throw a series of random letters together and hope the computer accepts them as an actual word.

WORK: What we do to put bread on the table. Usually white bread. And not the Country Hearth® stuff, either. No. We're talking the long-ass loaves of thinly sliced cardboard that are one step away from school paste but usually end up on the bargain rack at three for a dollar. There, you happy now, entrenched, grinding system of soulless capitalism?

WORKAHOLIC: A person who is addicted to work in the same way that any substance abuser is addicted to their drug of choice. And believe me, if work could be drunk, shot up, or snorted, these idiots would be all over it.

WORKOUT: One's regimen of vigorous exercise. Rendered entirely ineffective unless done behind giant health-club windows that allow passing pedestrians to watch you crushing it.

WORKPLACE: Ancient Rome, with a break room.

WORLD, THE: What most idiots assume involves only them and maybe six of their close friends. If they have six of them.

WORRY: The most deliciously tantalizing waste of time known to mankind.

WORTHY: What each of us needs to feel if we are to achieve emotional wholeness. Unfortunately, letting people know you are on a quest for emotional wholeness goes a long way toward making you more worthy of ridicule than anything else.

WRITER: A talented, sexy person made sexier by the way he works with sexy words to be super-sexy while creating a sexy mock dictionary and becoming all the more sexy because of it. Just saying.

WTF: Acronym for *What the Eff?* and a case study in how the taboo quality of an obscenity is completely denuded by reducing it to a single letter. Hence, you are not at all surprised that your staunchly conservative grandmother has been gleefully including a WTF in all her emails.

XBOX: Popular video game console that, much like its counterparts PlayStation® and GameCube™, was clearly invented by someone who wanted their children to vanish for hours on end.

XENOPHOBE: One who is irrationally frightened of foreign people or things. Unfortunately, there is no corresponding word to denote people who are justifiably frightened of xenophobes. ("Discerning"? "Sensible"?)

X-RAY: The other word that sort of begins with "x" that is used to take up space in sparsely populated sections of mock dictionaries.

YARD SALE: Event held in the hope that several idiots will show up by dusk to drop a few bucks on everything you were getting ready to throw away.

YEARBOOK: The high school and college version of the wedding photo album that you will not only never look at again, but also will gradually move to less and less conspicuous locations in your domicile.

YELP®: Your opportunity to have that damn coffee shop shut down just because they sold you a dry poppyseed muffin that one time.

YESTERDAY: The day before today, the past. Remember, yesterday is gone, and tomorrow is not yet here. So if right now really sucks, I don't know what to tell you.

YODA: Diminutive *Star Wars* character, trainer of Jedi knights and spouter of ersatz ancient philosophy, most famously "Do or do not, there is no try." Now, there is a fine piece of new-age crap that has messed up those of us who have done nothing but try for more years than it has taken the *Star Wars* franchise to run itself into the ground.

YOLO:

ACRONYM FOR *YOU ONLY LIVE ONCE,* AND PRETTY MUCH AN ANNOYING INVITATION TO VIOLENTLY END THE LIVES OF THOSE WHO SAY IT, THEREBY PROVING THE VALIDITY OF THE ACRONYM.

YOU: The one person no one else could be better at being. So if the best you can manage is a sort of half-assed, mediocre version of you, don't sweat it.

YOU FEEL ME?: Rhetorical question asked to engender a spirit of camaraderie-based empathy that somehow keeps managing to sound like an invitation to a fondling party.

YOU GOT THIS: Words of encouragement spoken to the players at Little League baseball games in order to let them know that they do not, nor are they likely to ever, actually have this.

YOUNG: Hated by everyone who has the misfortune of being even six lousy months above your age group.

YOUR/YOU'RE: Common spelling error that confuses "you are" with the possessive form "your." An easy way to remember how to use these words correctly is to not be an idiot.

YOUR BACK: What you foolishly think those six or eight very close of friends of yours will have in times of crisis. Whatever you need to believe.

YOUTUBE: What happened when somebody who was clearly not an idiot realized that every idiot thinks they have something to say.

ZEN: Japanese school of Mahayana Buddhism. An incredibly complex, meditative approach to enlightenment through the elimination of a consciousness of one's self. And it would make Zen masters furious to know that we have reduced it to such pastimes as "zenning out" on a sunset or a TV show. Well, that is *if* a Zen master was even *capable* of being furious, since they are so zenned out all the time. Lucky bastards.

ZERO: Nothing. Naught. Nil. And what my sorry-assed life has pretty much amounted to, let's face it. Sorry, did I say that out loud? Of course I didn't say it out loud; this is a book. Phew. That was close.

ZOMBIE: A no-longer-living being that is hell-bent on sucking out your brains so that it may continue to exist. Hey, aside from the no-longer-living part, isn't that your boss/spouse/parent/toxic friend/pretty much anyone?

ZOMBIE APOCALYPSE: An event that sounds so freaking cool, you just know that we idiots will pretty much will it into being.

ZOO: A place where majestic endangered species are saved and allowed to live out their lives as captive, moribund, gawked-at majestic endangered species.

ABOUT THE AUTHOR

In his mind, James Napoli divides his time between Paris, New York, and London. In reality, he divides his time between resenting the concept of work and obsessing about the wrong things. He claims to be the author of several humor books, including Sterling Innovation's *The Official Dictionary of Sarcasm*, but only when his loved ones demand some small scrap of evidence that he has amounted to anything.